Pre-Spanish Philippines

JUANA JIMENEZ PELMOKA, PH. D.

PHILIPPINES

Pearl of the orient seas.
Main Club, Camp John Hay
Baguio City, Philippines

Oh beloved Philippines fondly called Pearl of the
   Orient Seas.

In the abyss of thy bottomless seas.

Our truths are swallowed up in thee.

Only faith, the mighty faith the promise see.

An instant reminder of our ancient history.

Truths are on hand

The battle is in the mind

More to read, more to learn.

With humility I dedicate this book to the people of the Philippines and to my daughters. Elenita, Imelda, Sonia, Josefina and Teresita, in loving memory of my husband Atty. Flaviano A. Pelmoka of Muñoz, Nueva Ecija, Philippines.

Juana Jimenez Pelmoka (Ph.D Lit.)

"You cannot be wise without some
bases of knowledge, but you may
easily acquire knowledge and
remain bare of wisdom."

-ALFRED NORTH WHITEHEAD, PHILOSOPHER

Comment:

Words are inadequate to express my gratitude and appreciation for being one of the selected readers of this excellent scenario — the beauty of our cultural heritage.

Indeed, this is an eye-opener a challenge especially to our young generation to ponder on the great sacrifice and wisdom of the author in producing and sharing with us the immense wealth of her book.

(Miss) Lucia A. Orejana
Actg. Principal, Muñoz, N.E.
Provincial High School, Muñoz, Nueva Ecija
Year 1971-1972

ACKNOWLEDGEMENT

I owe a debt of gratitude to my beloved husband, Atty. Flaviano A. Pelmoka, for his encouragement and support in making this book a reality.

I extend my sincere thanks to my daughters for their tireless efforts in research and to Atty. Alberto A. Laguia of Madrid Spain who solicitously guided me through completion of this book.

This book entitled, **The Pre-Spanish Philippines**, traces the great movement of the people of the ancient period as it wove the pattern of our civilization for the betterment of all people including our forefathers and the present generation.

TABLE OF CONTENTS

CHAPTER IV   Religion

CHAPTER V   Culture

CHAPTER VI   Agriculture, Industry & Commerce

CHAPTER VII   Social Habits, Music & Dances

PRE-SPANISH PHILIPPINES

PROLOGUE

A hundred years ago famous historians pioneered whole images of records about our ancient history and civilization. However, they did not successfully explain our pre-Spanish periods. What was the Philippines like before Ferdinand Magellan's arrival? What kind of culture did the Filipinos have before Hispanization? What traits pre-disposed them to easily assimilate western civilization in their ethnic fabric? This book provides clues to these fascinating questions.

"Few nations[1] have a history so confused like the pre-Spanish civilization of the Philippines," said Isabelo de los Reyes. [1] This is due to the scarcity of available materials and records. Chronicles of the Spanish and others were hardly considered a history in its technical terms. In a land where earthquakes and storms of apocalyptic proportions continuously transformed the landscape, hardly any record was preserved. During the more than 300 years of colonial rule records were vandalized and destroyed.

The Indostans, Celts and Syrians allegedly wrote their history; although to date they have yet to be validated. However, the Spanish colonizers of the Philippines nor the Asiatic Archipelago, including the Philippines, appear not to have written theirs.

The dearth of records is not surprising if we consider the historical development of every nation. It would not be strange if the Romans had theirs after the Second Punic Wars, five hundred forty years after the founding of Rome, according to Fabio Pictor, Rome's antique historian. If the ancient civilizations of the world, the Romans, Greeks and Septentrionals who taught us their grandeur, did not have their history until Gregorio de Tours, it is therefore not strange that the Philippines, nestled in the vast and multi-racial Asiatic Archipelago, would not have theirs.

---

[1] Isabelo de los Reyes, **History of the Philippines.**

It is a fact that civilization does not occur in a day, a month, a year or from a sudden event, but rather through gradual providential developments over a period of time. Almost two thousand years have passed and yet our ancient civilization remains a paradox. Unfortunately there are no masses of artifacts nor volumes of documents available to guide us. We hope that some day a manuscript will satisfactorily chronicle whence and where the intricate fibers of courtesy, faith, morality and compassion were woven into the Philippine canvas. Such admirable traits remain-embedded in the Filipino tradition to this day.

Although our pre-Spanish history was chronicled by our colonizers, and thus inevitably depicted through their lenses those writings, nevertheless gave us insight into the Filipino archtype, the rhythm of his life, beliefs, customs and practices, his transition from nomadic life to urbanity.

Whence and how did the early Filipino become inherently civilized? For centuries the answers to these questions had been conjectures and contentions.

An ancient archipelago shaped by volcanic and tectonic activities over fifty million years ago, the Philippines consists of seven thousand islands. Originally connected by land bridges to the Asian continent, its coastline emerged when the sea rose and the landshelf disappeared at the end of the Ice Age.[2] Archaeological explorations in Palawan, Philippines, implied that it was joined with Malaysia in 45,000 to 50,000 B.C. at 30 meters below sea level.[3]

Sitting at the intersection of the Pacific Ocean, South China Seas and the Sulu Seas, it was a main hub for sea traders.[4] Accessible from all directions and alluring to foreigners because of its rich natural resources, the Philippine archipelago became a benevolent host to a potpourri of cultures as early as the 9th century and thus began the evolution of its own unique culture.

---

[2] H. Otley Beyer et al., **Pictorial History of the Philippines**, Capitol Publishing House, 1953.
[3] Fairbridge, **Tabon Cave, Palawan, Philippines,** 1962.
[4] National Geographic Magazine, Washington D.C., July 1986.

The Philippines had its own culture before the arrival of the Spaniards. People from Arabia, India and China sailed to the Philippines, vigorously traded goods and infiltrated the local culture. When Magellan and his expedition arrived in 1521, they found an economically vibrant culture. The Spanish colonizers wrote about the great number of stonewares, potteries and silk found in the area.

In recent years archaeologists unearthed tangible records which chronicled the birth and growth of our ancient civilization. Contemporary archaeological findings in other lands offered substantial explanations of external influences which shaped our culture.

Excavations of ancient graves produced burial jars, which experts dated at 91 B.C.. These testimonials from antiquity indicated Hindu and Chinese influences.[5]

The 1978 archaeological findings of gold in Bactria, north of Afghanistan" shed the lights of eventful decades many thousand years between the West and the East where so many different objects from many different cultures — Chinese mirrors, Roman coins, daggers from Siberia — had been found together in one situ".[6]

Two thousand years ago the Bactrian Plain served "as an important crossroad in the Silk Route of sea traders from the lands of the Roman Empire in the West to the Chinese cities protected by the Great Wall in the East."[7] Examination of the artifacts found in Bactria placed habitation of the area in the beginning of the second millennium B.C. and most importantly, it highlighted the Bactrians' love affair with Greco-Hellenistic traditions.

Through similar ancient sea trade routes, Hellenistic cultural influences travelled to Asia and inevitably reached Philippine shores. This explains the variegated ethnic threads interwoven in the Philippine cultural fabric.

---

[5] Fairbridge, **Tabon Cave, Palawan, Philippines.**
[6] National Geographic Magazines, **The Golden Hoard of Bacteria,** by Victor Ivanovich, Vol. 177, No. 3, March, 1990.
[7] Ibid.

There existed some groups who preferred to duel in an ethnic canopy, where they nurtured their old world customs and insulated themselves from the influence of the new ideologies. The early moralizing authors found no reason to laud the magnificent progress of our ancient people. However, much to our chagrin we give obeisance to those who reproved the negativism of their peers.

Historians have come and gone, but one wonders whether in general those authors, prior to embarking in their writings, tragically underestimated or completely missed the influence of the global diaspora of the Greek culture called Hellenism which was begun by Alexander the Great (336-323 B.C.) as it swept through the whole Eastern world.[8] This culture was further enhanced by the Roman conquest of Greece. Its influence encouraged unlimited cultural growth and finally ended the Dark Ages of Medieval Europe.

We consider that one of the endless truths and twists, millions of years ago, rested on the root stock given by Alexander the Great (336-323 before the Christian era). One who has a keen interest in geopolitics and economics should have a bird's eye view of this feat, where the Roman empire on its golden age played a great role on its spread; bore a continuing relation to the world especially Europe and more significantly to the Philippines.

We present the following excerpts which we feel we are particularly indebted to.

The Empire of Alexander the Great[9]

Some centuries ago before the birth of Christ, Alexander the Great (336-323 B.C.) conquered an enormous empire which comprised the whole of the known Eastern

[8] Monsignor Enrico Galbiate, The Early Church in the Acts of the Apostles with the Voluntary Workers of "MIMEP". In 36 B.C. Alexander the Great conquered the eastern world – Greece, Syria, Egypt and Persia. – nations of heterogeneous customs, religion, habits and language. Which he merged into one civilization called Hellenism. When Alexander died in 323 B.C. the Seleucids of Seria and Ptolemies of Egypt spread the Hellenistic culture through the whole East.

[9] The early Church in the acts of Apostles by Msgr. E. Galbiate page 20, 21.

world, Macedonia, Greece, Syria, Persia and Egypt, so he became the great monarch, venerated as god. But the people he governed were quite different in habits, customs, language and religion. In order to rule them better, he dreamt of merging them into one people, that of Greece. But it was only in the time of his successors, the Seleucids of Seria and the Ptolemies of Egypt, that the Greek culture spread through the East with the exception of Judea whose people, though subjected to its influence, preserved its ancient culture.

HELLENISM

The best men of Greece were thus scattered throughout the kingdoms of Asia Minor, the Middle East and Egypt, bringing a new impetus to the cultures and economic activities of the vast empire. The whole Eastern basin of the Mediterranean saw the flowering of a new civilization which had the common features in as much as each kept to the same Greek culture as if to a pattern.

This was characterized by the pursuit of art and a special interest on philosophical reflection, particularly with regards to moral and religious problems. This civilization was appropriately called Hellenism.

In 144 B.C. the Romans conquered Greece, but the civilization and culture of the vanquished country conquered the conquerors. Thus Hellenism was extended to Rome itself and illuminated also those western regions which were under Roman rule. Political unification favored religious unification. But with the coming of Hellenism, religion acquired a more intimate and profound character also: men felt more intensely the problem of their moral life and their fate after death, and their minds were therefore prepared to welcome Hellenism.

As the centuries marched on, many traditional narratives of episodes became parts of history and changed the outlook of the world. Hellenism's dramatic effect is indelibly etched in our civilization.

Due to the difficulties of getting original materials from Manila we used chronicles and annals from the National Library of Madrid, Spain, some periodicals from the Middle East, the United States and Manila.

In our research of this Bibliography, we found conflicting materials which showed the following common threads:

(a) discrepancies in style and contentions which degraded the pre-Spanish civilization of the Philippines;

(b) The persistence of some authors in using the words barbaric and uncivilized;

(c) authors based their datas on already existing institutions such as those of the Graeco-Romans which had already influenced our forefathers.

(d) Early institutions formed by the Pre-Spanish Philippines were analogous with those of the Graeco-Roman institutions of the Medieval period of the West.

The history of nations demonstrate how each one passes from a period of barbarism to a period of urbanity. Barbarism in antiquity has no meaning or significance from the standpoint of humanity at large unless it is contrasted with the civilized ways or urban life of the different ethnic groups.

Historical occurrences will be meaningless, if authors fail to capture the electrifying atmosphere of the cultural development of a people; thus defeating the principle of man's inherent character for survival and growth as typical of a rational being.

In the book of Napoleon Hill, Law of Success, he said, "By far the most important of a man's make-up comes through the law of social heredity; this term refers to the method by which one generation imposes upon the minds of the generation under his control, the beliefs, legends and ideas which were inherited by the following generations."[10]

Recent archaeological findings confirm that by the time of the

---

[10] Napoleon Hill, **Law of Success**, page 17.

first arrival of the Spaniards in the Philippines, it had already passed the Period of Barbarism imputed to our ancient forefathers.[11]

Isabelo de los Reyes offered his opinion when he said, "It seems easy and incontrovertible; it is also certain that there is no case more debatable than the filiation of the Philippine inhabitants." He continued to say that, "Much has been said and written about this and dispelled many errors some so rare."[12]

We do not negate but acknowledge that the problem arises from the inherently complex process involved in researching the truth. We believe the early authors who dwelt on the Barbaric Period of the Philippines should have proceeded with caution, mindful that historical suppositions are easily labeled as facts.

Martinez de Zuniga cited an example, "Authors always accepted what was marvelous and divided the inhabitants in various styles; their histories did not lack men with tails and satiro man to arouse sensation in the human manner."

Nevertheless, we find comfort in the thought "that facts are man-made; they are just distorted by the eyes that formed them or they were meant to be weapons of ridicule."

However, the narrative descriptions of the structural formation of our past gave us courage and inspiration to tackle this work. We honor the historical authors with gratitude for we consider these records not only legal documents of our ancient past but also a complete blueprint of unimpeachable sources rigorously approved by modern ethnographical science.

---

[11] David Howard Bain, **Sitting in Darkness**, page 109. The people of the Philippines already had a rich and varied culture when the Spaniards arrived in the Philippines.

[12] Isabelo de los Reyes., **History of the Philippines.**

Husking Rice This procedure is no longer followed, but has been superseded by rice mills.

Chapter I

GENERAL VIEW OF THE PRE-SPANISH CIVILIZATION

We enunciate this chapter as the base of our work to determine the finality to which all chapters will be anchored. Without this description it would be difficult to understand its inherent peculiarity and phenomenal development.

We researched and segregated the historical sources to resolve what experts considered as a conflict of origin. The following epigraphs shed light to the missing chapters of our ancient civilization:

A. THE ANTIQUE NAMES

This topic properly introduces the decades preceding the study of the Philippines' pre-Spanish civilization.

It is common knowledge that all things and events have corresponding names.

Research on the end of the pre-Spanish civilization proved easy; research on its beginning was to the contrary in as much as it required a fundamental, qualitative and in-depth research using authentic sources.

When did Philippine civilization begin? Dr. Otley Beyer cited 3000 B.C. based on archeological discoveries.[13]

The names given to the Philippines are pivotal to our work. For if the antique names were known in ancient times by the Greeks, Romans and Egyptians, its existing civilization and prevailing culture could be presumed.

The early inhabitants named places after geographical routes, descriptions, anecdotal observations customs and traditions. They derived names literally from such determining factors. None of the

---

[13] **Prehistory by Galang,** Encyclopedia of the Philippines, Vol. II, pp 21-26.

authors of antiquity, nor the Filipino authors, wrote about the antique names given to the Philippines.

Other cultures could have reached far places as Tarsito observed.[14] It could also happen that with the great geographical knowledge of the epoch, civilized people could have described the civilization as barbaric or a flowering civilization. Marginal early historical writings did not allude to the pre-Spanish Philippine civilization, except for Ptolome in his celebrated Tables.[15] He believed that there were three islands called Maniolas whose people built ships using wooden pegs instead of iron which they called "Iman" (magnet). They believed that magnets detained their ships.

Father Collin was the first historian who believed that the Philippines was the Maniolas referred to by Ptolome.

The navigators of the time believed that those islands ought to be in the Gulf of India in the Peninsula of Gold. They therefore believed that Ptolome did not know the place or its existence.[16] On the contrary he believed that the land of Sumatra faced west and was joined with the fixed land of Africa. Father Murillo investigated this in disbelief.

Father Fernandez Navarette argued it with good reasons as follows:

Manila, an area of stagnant water and marshy land,was a tongue-shaped peninsula. The Tagalogs gave it its name. In like manner the port of Cavite was called Cavit because the land had the shape of a hook. Malate was called such because of salt found in the land. Manila as it is known today is in its original location. Father Collin could not be mistaken because he was a Tagalog minister in Manila. Santa Ines considered the etymology of Fernandez to be more antique because it had an etymological

---

[14] Ibid.

[15] Claudio Ptolomeo was Greek astronomer and geographer who flourished in the second century A.D. His tables showed some islands called *Maniolas* or *Barusas*, which were believed to be the Philippines by some authors like F. Collin and Mercator. Other authors insisted them to be Liquios or Luzon.

[16] Ibid. I

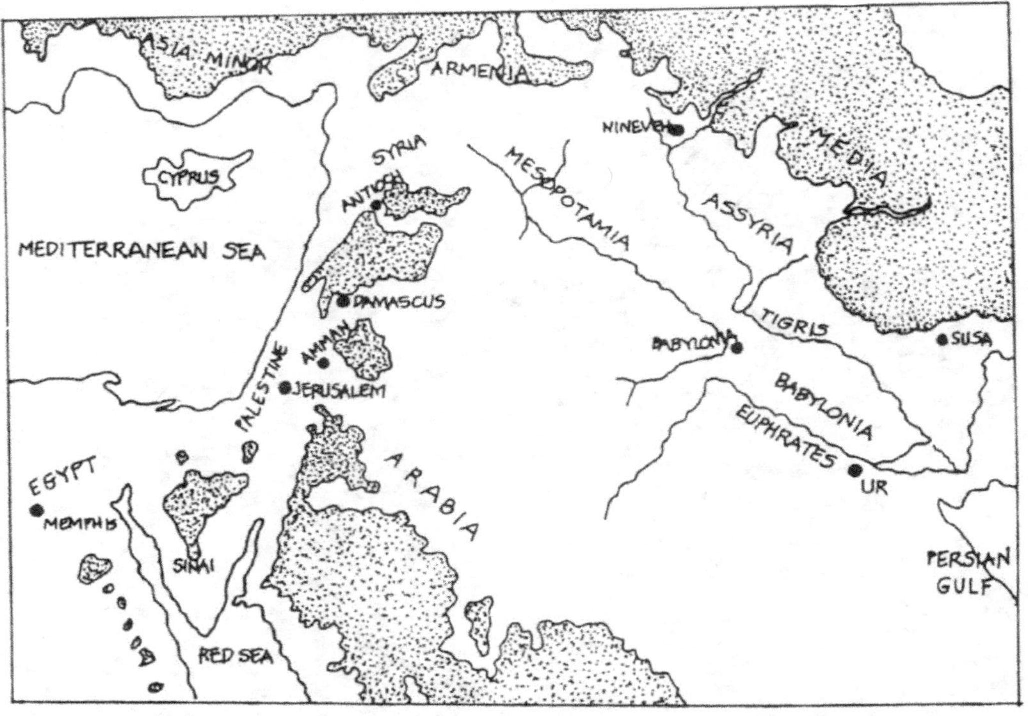

The Extent of Ancient Civilization

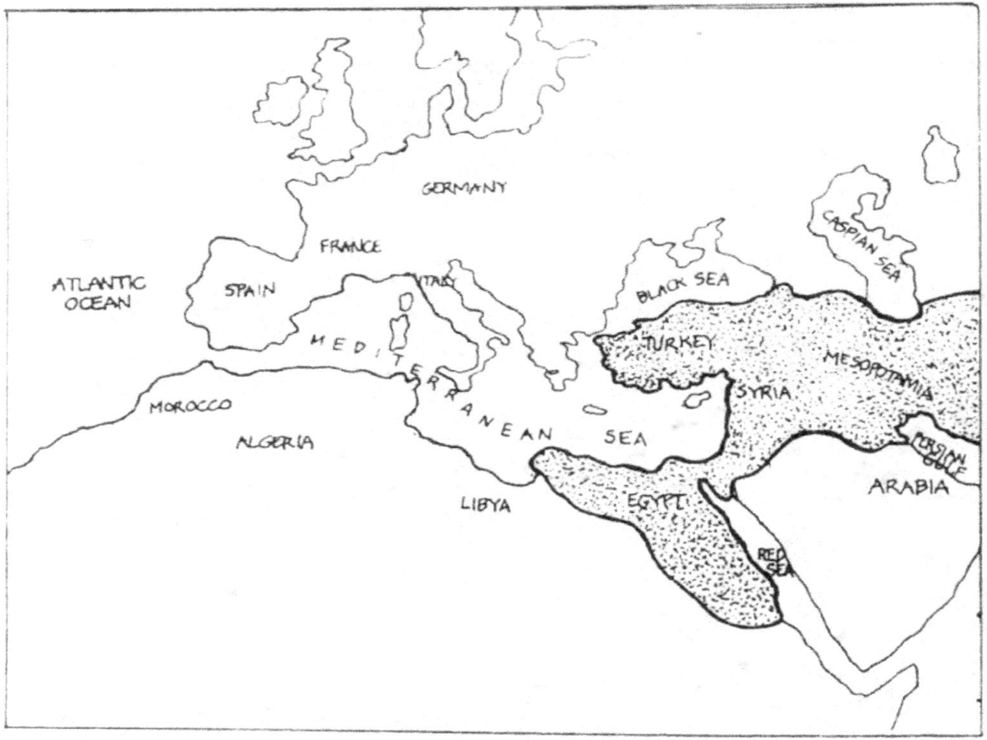

The Empire of Alexander the Great

The Philippines and Its Neighboring Countries

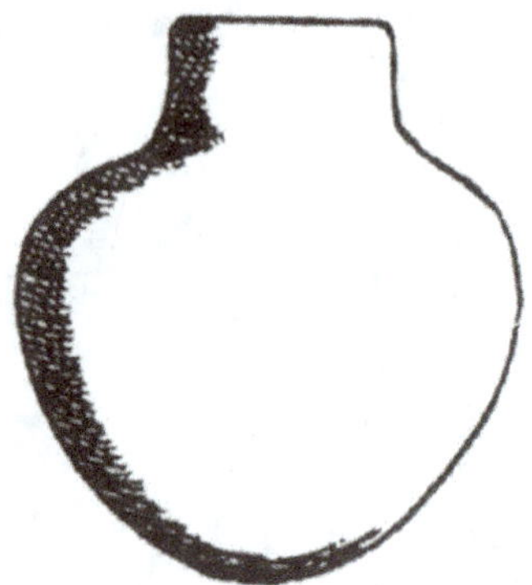

a) From Diwata Cave, an example of a **Tabon Polished** vessel with highly polished red slip. It has a tall and narrow neck.

d) Another example of **Tabon Polished** – It is a bowl with a well defined rim that is canted inward. It is a very simple form.

e) One more example of the **Tabon Incised** style – This pot is from the Duyong Cave. It exhibits the same type of craftsmanship and the design as the others previously shown.

b) **Tabon Incised** – An example from Diwata Cave, a squat clay bowl, with wide opening, decorated with crude chevron pattern running continuously on the upper part of the vessel.

c) From Diwata cave, an example of medium high clay pot, with inward tapering upper body, richly decorated with chevron patterns forming elongated diamond forms in the middle. The lower part of the vessel is covered with paddle impressed design.

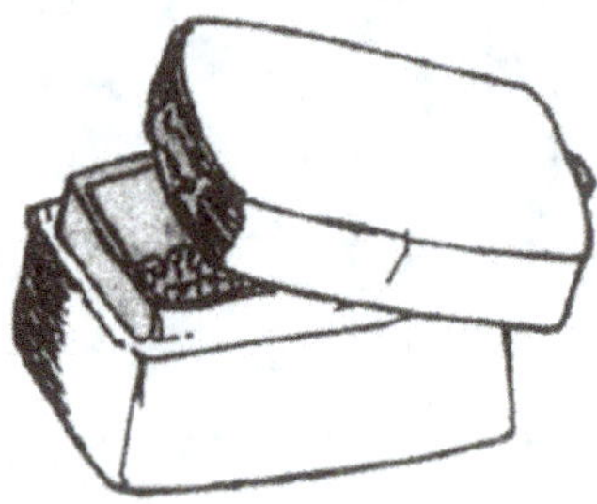

f) Another example of a pottery container is this unusually shaped box that contained painted teeth of several persons. It was excavated from Bato Puti cave.

Examples from the Tabon Diggings of forms of potteries with decor elements.

Tagalog diction which were: "May" and "Nila" and referred to by others as "May" and "Dila". During the time of the early settlers, folklore told a story about an islet shaped like a tongue in the middle of a river by the mouth of the sea. They called this tongue-shaped islet "Meydila", which meant a place where there was a tongue. In Tagalog, "may" means "there" and "dila" means "tongue". With the passage of time the islet washed away to the sea. The word "Meydila" was probably corrupted and became "Maynila". According to some inhabitants Manila was named after the Nila tree found in the place. However, this was not quite a believable story since no such tree withstood the passage of time.

Neither author could prove his story. There was no proof that the early settlers used wooden pegs in their ships. Neither the Maniolas of Ptolome nor the inhabitants of the islands of Mindanao, Borneo, Madagascar and others used wooden pegs to build their ships.

F. Delgado said that F. Collin called it Luzon. He took this from the etymology and catalogue of the "pilon" which was a tool for polishing rice, their common food. He said that it would not be out of context if the whole Asiatic peninsula would be called "Luzon"or "Luzonica" because they all used "pilon" in husking their rice. Nevertheless, it could be called Luzon but it must come from a nobler source. [17] This pilon used by the natives to husk their rice was called "Luzong" in their idiom.

If this could be sufficient reason to call the islands Luzon after the pilon they used to husk their rice, then all the islands in the entire Asian continent which used pilon would have been called "Luzon" or "Luzonica".

What was admirable about this author and celebrated historian was his attraction to drawing the pilon as if he had not seen it in the form of a chalice in Europe or in the Indies where they in fact could be found in different forms and shapes. In this case the name Luzon cannot come from this etymology of rice and tools that removed its husks which were common in Asia and the Gandes.

---

[17] Retana. **Apartado Bibliographo,** p. 36

The real etymology of the name Luzon was not the pedestrian one cited by F. Collin and other provincial historians. The ethmology must have come from a more precious tool and not from the "pilon," a crude mortar used in Asia to husk [18] their common food.

The Spaniards adopted the name "Luzon" from the Chinese who came to the islands in their boats to trade gold, pearls and fruits. Other Chinese merchants called the island Luzon, which was somewhat similar to "Sunson", a place in China where they came from. It signified fixed land. Thus the Chinese traders came to Luzon from Sunson. The Spaniards heard this name frequently from the Chinese merchants and also began to call the island Luzon. [19] The natives used Luzon when they communicated with the Spaniards. Thus this name had a better origin than those theorized by the historians.

This conformed to the book Conquista by Reverend Historian Gaspar de San Agustin where he named the Islands "Manila". Other authors who called this island Luzon were Dr. Morga, and Agensola.

The opinion of Mercator was not proven to be true. The following names were given:

"Insulae placeris seu brevium", it was the name according to the opinions of Pedro Apiano and Gemma Pusio.[20]

But the same F. Dias disagreed that those islands were really the Philippines.

"Lequios" by F. Murillo Velarde.

"Celebes" or Celibes. According to F. Grijalva, the Philippines was already called as such before Villalobos dominated the Islands. Celebes was an error of Grijalva according to F. Collin and San Antonio.[21]

"Islas de Cebu", Islands of Cebu, was the name given by Magellan and his men who fought the natives. Here we see that the

---

[18] F. Delgado, **Historia de Filipinas**, p.11, cap. II.
[19] Ibid
[20] Conquesta - Casimiro Dias, page 23.
[21] Murillo Velarde Geografico (1) Grijalva

author took a part for the whole and got the name Manila or Cebu after the discovery of Magellan.[22]

"Archipelago of San Lazaro". This name had been used by many authors according to the diary of Albo and the concurrence of Pigafetta. This was the first positive name of the Philippines.

"Filipinas", the name given by Rui Lopez de Villalobos in 1543 to honor the memory of Philip II when he was prince of Austria. [23]

"Islas de Poniente", an unfortunate conquest.

"Islas de Oriente" was given by the Portuguese.

M. Haberlandt explained that under the dominion of the air, in the physical medium that surrounded us were a series of external powerful conditions like climate, geographical situation, territorial structure, economic movement, etc.

Parallel to this natural medium, appearing as an important analogical factor, was the cultural medium, which encountered situation of human groups. Thus it can be said that climate and geographical situation of people influenced half of their destiny and the historical base where it rested constituted the other half.

The idea of man, the individual, or as part of a social group, depended in many respects on the natural surrounding he had converted into a common place.

Haberlandt continued to say that the climate, the geographical situation, and its physical aspects, and the biological ethnic groups were under the dominion of natural influences. The animal and vegetable kingdom depended on latitude and climate, and here the influence was at the same time generalized and profound in all.[24]

B. GEOGRAPHICAL DESCRIPTION

(a) Historical Introduction:

Many authors debated over the names of the ancient Philippine

---

[22] Grijalva - Geografia pages 3-4
[23] Ibid
[24] M. Haberlandt, **Etnografia**, pp. 30-31

archipelago if Ptolome's conjecture in his famous geographical tables were correct, that those islands were indeed the Philippine archipelago, the authors of antiquity could have described its flowering civilization.

The New World's[25] first knowledge about the Philippine archipelago came from Pigafetta's account of Magellan's expedition.

Ironically, the objective of Magellan's expedition was not for the discovery of the Philippines since the Spaniards did not even know of its existence. The Spanish Crown commissioned Magellan to sail to the Spice Islands which were being exploited by the Portuguese. The conflict between Spain and Portugal over the Spice Islands, or Molucas, resulted in the famous "Bula" of Pope Alexander IV on May 14, 1493.

In an effort to settle the territorial disputes between Portugal and Spain, Pope Alexander IV authored an agreement between the two countries that would cut the world in two with an imaginary line running north to south in the western Atlantic. This agreement was called the "Bula" or the Treaty of Tordesillas.[26]

Magellan's expedition for the Spice Islands or the Molucas, using the sea route which they thought had been ceded to them by the "BULA", followed a different route from those used by the Portuguese, sailing west to get to the east, navigating on what they thought to be Spain's jurisdictional waters in order to avoid conflict with the Portuguese. [27]

With this antecedent they navigated oceans of the world and after enumerable sacrifices and heroic efforts, Magellan and his surviving crew arrived in Philippine archipelago.

Accidentally found

Geonology unknown

But the Holy Spirit was home

---

[25] Father Collin - Labor Evangelica page 36

[26] Encyclopedia Britanica 1954

[27] Boletin de la Sociedad Geografica, Madrid 1876, T.I. p. 301.

18

The spectacular discovery by the Spanish expedition disclosed a land of singular beauty, wealth and a flowering life, which they thought to be the recompense for the heroic efforts and sacrifices of the sailors and navigators. This was the first circum-navigation of the globe.[28]

Magellan sailed in waters never sailed before by any of the European explorers of his time. His goal to find the Spice Islands turned out to be a voyage of discovery of the Philippines. Because of this the Spaniards claimed that they were the ones who discovered the Philippines and the first to bring it to light before the rest of Europe. News about all aspects of life in the archipelago, its vast natural wealth and beauty, its geographical location and most important of all its civilized and friendly people spread about in Europe.

(b) Situation-Limits and Extension:

We commence this paragraph with the mention of some authors who contributed much to the compiling of the great geographical and cartographical composition of the Philippine Archipelago.

The Philippine archipelago is situated in the torrid zone between 4° and 2° 10' North latitude and 160° 40' and 126°34' East latitude of Greenwich.

It is of rigorous justice for a modern investigator to have accumulated and presented records on this vast subject. We thank our teachers who preceded us in geographical descriptions, if there were errors* it could be due to the imperfect precision instruments used in those times. We give admiration and gratitude for the remembrance of some authors like Claudio Montero, Alfonso de Buisa, Rivadenier, Grijalva, F. Collin, Chirino, Murillo, Velarde and others too numerous to name them all.

According to established geographical and cartographical compositions, the Philippine Archipelago forms part of the numerous chains of mountains drawing out of the Kamchatka peninsula at the extreme North East end of Asia; with its Oriental Coast

---

[28] F. Collin, **Labor Evangelica**

touching the dominion of Kuriles, Japan, Formosa, and the Molucas, extending as far as to the extreme ends of Australia. The Archipelago is defined by its occidental coastal boundaries. The limits of the China Sea serve as a barrier from the pounding water of the Pacific Ocean. [29]

At the time of the Spaniards' arrival the Philippine archipelago, consisted of only 4,000 islands. Due to volcanic activities over an extended period of time, different islands rose above sea level and the archipelago grew to its present composition of 7,000 or more islands.[30] The most important among them are Luzon, Visayas, and Mindanao, a cluster of islands adjacent to Jolo.

The Philippines coasts are generally rugged and irregular, surrounded by beaches of white sand and coral reefs and at many points by dangerous cliffs. The Eastern part offers safe shores but the anchorage is frequently exposed to the violent waves of the Pacific Ocean.

The maximum extension of the archipelago is 1,950 kilometers from south to north; 1,284 from east to west. Its total area of 2,961 square kilometers is larger than Great Britain, half of France and two thirds of the Iberian Peninsula.[31] Its total coastline is twice as long as the entire coastline of the United States.

The interior waters of the archipelago are difficult to navigate due to the forceful current from the sea, as its waves lash forth through inner passages and canals, running along the coastal configuration, producing treacherous currents. In the Straits of Surigao between Leyte and Mindanao, the velocity of the currents sometimes rises up to 15 kilometers per hour.

The world' deepest ocean floor is located northeast of the Mindanao shores.

---

[29] Claudion Montero, Opinion cite, p. 29
[30] Courtesy of The Department of National Defense
Bureau of Coast and Geodetic Survey 1950
[31] Jose Montero Vidal, El Archipelago Filipino, p. 38
115, 707 Sq. miles- Great world atlas p.128.

(c) Geology:

The Philippines' geological frame of mountain ranges, hills, valleys and plains mimics a landscape predominant in Asia.

For centuries historians believed that the Philippines was a part of the Asian mainland. Recent archaeological excavations in the Philippines proved this belief to be true.

The geological structure of the Philippine archipelago appears to be incomplete. Masses of land formed from volcanic rocks of long ago, continue to change the archipelago's terrain. The 7,000 islands stretched along the Pacific historically and figuratively had served as stepping stones for its Asian neighbors – Borneo, Java, Sumatra, Celebes, Malaysia, Polynesia in the east, New Zealand in the south and the Marianas.

Coins in various forms were found in Binangonan in the island of Luzon near the Pacific Coast. The old and new fossils were lacking in places of high altitude. In the Northern part of the Gulf of Davao an adverse movement was observed; the land went down from the dying forest invaded by the sea.

This book of our pre-Spanish civilization compiles chronicles and annals of our past and presents relevant records which may open the secrets of the obscure background of the Philippine archipelago. Included here are the influences of the old Greek and Graeco-Roman civilization which are deeply rooted in our culture.

One of the most priceless and significant archaeological findings in the Philippine archipelago were the fossils of homo sapien men who arrived from the Asian mainland through land bridges during the Pleiestocene or Ice Age. Homo sapiens were composed of different races: the Caucasoid, Africans, and Asians. We interpret this as a divine event, heralding the Philippines' destiny to be the cradle of Christian belief in Asia, a significant part of a providential plan to save men.[32]

In this archaeological discovery it established that the Philippines was a part of the Asian mainland in the remote past and that

---

[32] Msgr. Enrico Galbiate. **The History of Salvation in the Old Testament,** p. 23 h

its people had its own culture thousand of years before Spanish colonization as chronicled by the scholar, Howard Bain:

> "The people and culture of the Philippine archipelago was already rich and varied stew when the Spaniards arrived. The archipelago had been inhabited by humans at least twenty thousand years, a figure established with the discovery in 1962 of fossilized skullcap in the Southwestern part of Palawan Islands; tectites and tools from the Pleistocene era have been found in many places around the islands and the depth-age estimate placed these at fifty thousand years. The most popular theory suggests that during the Pleistocene epoch the level of the ocean was lower by some 156 feet, which exposed a broad low land where the South China Sea now exists; across these land bridges, wandered the first inhabitants of the Philippines as well as those of Malaysia and the Indo China. Later after the earth's ice cap retreated and brought the exposed land masses to their present configuration where the South China Sea is, other settlers and traders arrived by boat from Malaysia, Indo-China, China, Borneo and even India, contributed to the pre-colonial life which was primarily agriculture, though trade flourished among the Western Pacific islands and with the Asian mainland.[33]

Let there be no doubt in any mind,
That All-wise Providence had reached our land,
And had molded us to be man.
Pause on the margin of these momentous acts.
For God's message had reached us.
Be grateful for these Providential happenings,
Which headed to the divinity that shaped our ends.
But we often wished that we would clearly read
God's signal He had conveyed.

[33] Howard David Bain, **Tabon Cave**
The place chosen by God for revealing Himself and unfolding the history of salvation, was at the meeting point of the great civilization of the Middle East and stretched to the coast of the Mediterranean Empire in Macedonia under Alexander and the Romans. So in God's time His words would reach the East, Europe and Egypt at the same (32) – Enrico Galbiate History of Salvation p. 32.

(d) Volcanology:

The volcanos performed considerable influence in the territorial formation of the Philippine archipelago. However, the extent of this influence has not been precisely determined.

Its volcanic ranges are part of the Pacific system and are considered a continuation of the great Cordillera which runs north to south from Kuriles to New Zealand, passing through Japan, China's Hofei, Celebes and crossing other ranges under the Sea of India. The first link is the chain of the volcano of the Babuyan Islands, north of Luzon, and the Taal Volcano near Manila. The Cordillera is divided in two: the Oriental which forms Mayon and Bulusan, southwest of Luzon and the other is Occidental which has two volcanos, the Malaspina and Magaso in the Islands of Negros and Camiguin near the cost of Mindanao. These branches both joined the south of Mindanao and a group which belong to Calayo and the Apo which dominate the Gulf of Davao.[34]

The archipelago has twenty five volcanos, seventeen of which are active, like Mt. Pinatubo in Luzon which recently brought devastation to the islands.

The Philippines experiences frequent earthquakes, a continued period of fluctuation generally directed from west to east. Manila is frequently suffering from temblors caused by earthquakes like the eruptions of the Taal Volcano and other ones. The Islands of Polilio, located in the coast of Luzon, had a submerged volcano.

(e) Orography:

From the south of Mindanao to the north of Luzon, the general orographic system of the Philippine archipelago follows the same extended lines to the direction of the three series of islands, connecting the archipelago with the rest of Malaysia. Thus the mountains of Mindanao, more or less in the West and center, are a continuation of the two cordilleras separating Oriental Borneo

---

[34] Encyclopedia Universal España, Vol. 23, page 1, 346

and Celebes, only to merge again as groups in the waters of Jolo and Sanguin.[35]

The center of Jolo whose normal difference is Southeast to North East comprises all the occidental peninsula of Mindanao. At the center of Sanguin, expanding from South to North and gradually curving to the West and East of the mountain lines, there is another of the same character that overlooks the Pacific Ocean. This is extended to the Northwest in a curve that passes the Islands of Masbate, Ticao, Burias, in the East. It develops a parallel curve formed by the Island of Samar, the peninsula of Camarines and the islands of Polilio. On the other part Bohol, Negros, Cebu and Panay are at the center of the archipelago of Jolo or the parallel folds; at the end of Mindoro and Luzon are the extension of Palawan and Borneo. It is observed that the islands projecting and extensive are the islands off of Luzon that reunite all the cordilleras in the huge artistic Caraballo mountain that looks like an arch where all the points converge. All the archipelago lands are mountainous except the plains along the rivers.

The detailed topography of the islands is distinguished for its simplicity. All are longitudinally linked by mountains, like Negros, Leyte and Paragua.[36]

While the Cordillera of Panay is found near the coast of Bohol and Samar, it only had scattered heights and did not have a pattern. The major islands of Luzon show major variations on the surface.

The Oriental coast of Luzon is separated by an elevated mountain from the extreme northwest of Manila. On the west of that mountain sits the fertile valley of Cagayan and between it is the coast of the China Sea, bordered in the north by a series of mountains of 1500 to 1800 meters high and in the south from the Gulf of Lingayen to Manila Bay, a great level plain that is limited on the west by the Zambales mountain; its meridional part is cut by numerous mountains and volcanos.

---

[35] Ibid., p 1,3, x 6 y ss
[36] **Encyclopedia España** Vol. 23 p 1, , x 6 y ss

West of Mindanao the mountain faces the Pacific, opens to the valley of the Agusan River. This is the Apo Volcano rising at the height of 3200 meters, the highest point in the archipelago. To its west stands the Rio Grande of Mindanao.[37]

(f) Hydrography:

The small and narrow Cordillera presents the rugged back of the islands in its great and central division of its waters where it all cascades straight to the rivers and weakens to the seas.

The fluvial system of Luzon and Mindanao is complicated by the water distribution parallel the Cordilleras which permits the unfolding of considerable and extensive currents of the Rio Grande of Cagayan which courses down 3,500 kilometers to the open China Sea, north of the Islands. Another important waterway is the river Abra which leads to Vigan.

The rivers within the cost are few, shallow, thorny and short with the exception of Bohol. The rivers of Bohol are wide and deep, thus allowing navigation of small water crafts. The northwest end of the Bohol River unfolds 350 meters to the sea, contributing to the commercial life of the port in Dagupan.

The Pasig River has a course of only 20 kilometers, but it is an important commercial waterway because its route connects Laguna Bay to Manila Bay, the first and leading port of the Philippines.

The fluvial waters of Mindanao and its major part are determined by the parallel Cordillera and generally continue one direction north, west and south. It is easier to navigate than the waters of Luzon.

The Rio Grande of Mindanao, or Pulangui, collects its waters from the central depression of the islands and carries it to the occidental sea of Celebes. It is navigable by many ships through the lake of Agusan. The river of Agusan is formed 40 kilometers to the south coast, unfolding on the north coast and is navigable at a length of some kilometers.

---

[37] Ibid. p. 1345 y ss

The longest lake in the Philippines is in Laguna. Laguna Bay is 40 kilometers long and 18 kilometers wide, with Taal Volcano sitting at its center.[38]

(g) Climate:

Located in the torrid zone, the climate of the Philippine Archipelago is moderately hot and at times humid. As an island in the Asiatic continent with its peculiar topography, its climate is considered comfortably warm.

The calendar year is divided equally between the dry and wet seasons.

Generally the Philippine climate, like those of its neighbors, is under the influence of monsoons which determine the variations in temperatures. The rains and the winds are the forces that affect the navigation and agriculture of its people.

The Philippine topography is affected by two monsoons which create the dry and wet seasons. The storms and typhoons from the China Sea bring abundant rainfall between the months of July and December. The hardest rainfalls come between the months of July to September.

Typhoons which cross north of Manila from the eastern part of the archipelago—a vague surface running between 150 degrees and 145 degrees east latitude of Greenwich and between 5 degrees and 20 degrees north— are the most vicious until they eventually weaken as they reach the South China Sea. The storms were feared for its powerful double movement, a clockwise rotation, similar to a tornado, frequently creating disaster not only on land, as they uproot houses and destroy crops, but also at sea, as they cause shipwrecks. It was also observed that in some places tornados were frequent, although in short durations, knocking down electricity which sometimes causes fire. Tornados also create electrical storms with lightning flashing as frequently as 53 times per minute.

The dry season is hot and humid

As in other places, the development of the monsoons do not coincide with the equinox and do not simultaneously occur in all parts of the archipelago.[39] The rainy season begins until the middle of May. Rain showers occur more often starting in June. The temperature gradually falls, noticeably in the months of November to February. By December the wind direction comes from the southwest, a change, ushering the start of the dry season which prevails for the rest of the year.

Extreme atmospheric imbalances, such as alternating cyclones and storms, were frequent. They were not different from those of the oceanic Indian cyclones and Atlantic hurricanes.

Simple depressions occur between 4 degrees and 12 degrees north and differ from the more severe ones that occur between 16 degrees and 22 degrees parallel.

The low parallel occurs between December and March producing fresh winds.

(h) Plants:

Although the Philippine plants are similar to those of Malaysia, they are different in some respects.

Almost all the Philippine species are represented in the peninsula of Malaysia, in the islands of Zonda and in some parts of Australia.

All the proper species of the archipelago are rare and develop in a unique way.

At an altitude of 3,000 feet, the vegetation is like those of Borneo and the archipelago of Zonda. With an equatorial character in the north of Mindanao and Jolo, the vegetation weakens towards the northland and is no longer tropical.

The difference between the species were well marked according to regions. Vegetation in the Pacific cascade thrived in the rain while those found towards the China Sea thrived in dry, compact mountainous soil. Agriculture in these regions were limited to splendid virgin forests, ferns, orchids, palms, etc. Pine trees were

---

[39] **Encyclopedia España,** vol. 23

not found, except in Baguio.[40] The Philippine species were divided in thirteen groups: (1) Grains, beans, tubers, and gramineous; garden plants, textiles, oleaginous (oily), tinterea (for coloring), fecula (for starch), saccharin (like sugar), fruits, aromatics, medicinals, fruit trees, vegetable products, trees for decorations and maderable wood.

Gramineous products in agriculture such as rice, were found in the archipelago upon the arrival of the Spaniards. It was the most important food of the people in the islands, and they grow it in abundance.

Corn is also used for food by the people and their animals.

Cogon is a cane specie and like nipa and bamboo, were used for roofing houses. Wood was used for the construction of houses, boats, ships, baskets and furnitures.

Textiles – abaca was well esteemed due to the quality of its fibers. Cotton had three types – "Capas", "Buboy" and "Capasangly". The Philippine pineapple was more important as textiles than as fruits. Ramie fibers rival the flax. The Cabo Negro or Caong were used as strings for guitars. The Palasan with its length of 20 meters were used for the structural framework of the houses. They were also used for making hats and furnitures. With this system, they also used the "pandan", a buri palm and the shoots of the Elechos.

Legumes – Mongo, frijoles, patani, tomatoes, eggplants and watermelons.

Oleaginous – It is excellent for paints.

Fecula – Kangkong, camote, sago; they are sweet and contain alcohol.

Canes – was the source of sugar in the Philippines; had twenty varieties and was an important product of the islands. The nipa or "sasa"; were used as roof materials of houses for its cool effect. Its juice was used in the manufacture of brandy due to its strong spirit. Alcohol drinks were also manufactured from textiles.

---

[40] **Encyclopedia Universal,** Vol. 23 page 1345

Carabaos al baño

Aromatic Plants – The queen of the aromatic plants in the Philippines was the tobacco which was imported from Mexico in the sixteenth century.

Medicinal Plants – The Ricono, the Bocanal, were organic insecticides which killed head lice. The Salibutbut and the Pandacaque serve as iodine in stopping bleeding from cuts.

Fruit Trees – Mango, Lanzones and Champoy.

Vegetables – Papaya, varieties of bananas and six varieties of oranges.

Hard Wood – They have many kinds of hard wood, some of them are the following: Abilo, Acle, Parang, Agojo, Alacao, Narra, Apitong Camagong, Calumpani, Mulave, etc. These showed the wealth of the Philippine forestry.

(i) Animals:

There were disparities in the superior groups of animals found in Java, Sumatra, Borneo and Celebes. Their differences are measured in zoological scales.

It is noted for example that the Philippines did not have the orangutan, tiger, elephant, zebra, etc. No fierce animals were found in the archipelago. In exchange of the special forms, the Philippine animals were numerous and showed peculiar features inspite of the points of contact with the Malaysian regions.

Among the domestic animals found during the arrival of the Spaniards in the islands were carabaos, farm raised chickens, pigs and ducks. In the mountains were many birds, doves, Gauls. The Gauls sang during certain hours of the day just as the rooster crows to herald sunrise and sunset. A specie of the oyster had its shell made into water pitcher.[41]

(j) Natural Resources:

Because of the vast plant resources and the influence of the weather the islands produced extraordinary wealth in livestock.

---

[41] Historia General de Filipinas, p.13.

The first aborigines did not have to work for their food as they were readily available. This was a considerable factor in their long cultural development. The Filipinos already had a developed stage in agriculture. They capitalized the wealth of the soil as they extracted mineral substances from it, specially iron, which gave fame to the Philippine archipelago and launched its blossoming commerce.

They benefited from gold, amber pearls, tapers and wax. When the Spaniards arrived they had already exploited the different wealth of the archipelago. With the considerable natural wealth of the Philippine archipelago, its people inevitably developed their culture even before the Spaniards arrived.

(C) POPULATION AND RACES:

The Philippine archipelago, surrounded by numerous ancient beliefs as to its origin and name, eventually became known in many parts of the world as a united group of people "The only people enriched with the cultural ideals of Christian and modern civilization, it was considered the occidental oasis in those remote seas of the Far East."[42] Through the centuries of foreign dominion, their struggles and lives in the islands became known and respected.

Thus, the ancient authors began to write about the Philippines and struggled to find the answers to the scientific problems but failed. In general terms, it was a quest to compose a history of a nation in consonance with its actual discovery in 1521.

With this intention, we initiate this epigraph, for in no other title can we have a work of critical history.

In our investigation of the different authors who wrote about this subject, we studied first the modern and ancient authors who had no errors, who were more voracious, prestigious and enjoyed more authority.

---

[42] Encyclopedia Universal, Vol. 23, p. 1356

In relation to this work, we found many learned authors of different nationalities who spent their precious time in the ethnography of the Philippine archipelago, especially about the ancient ones. We have here the account of Montano who was especially commissioned by the French government to study the ethnography of the oriental races.

Many authors have said that Mallat has written a complete work about the Philippine ethnography. Other authors who had written about our Philippine ethnography were: Blumentritt the illustrious Filipinologist, Virchow, Bastian, H. Hary, Rosny and Mas.

We extended our gracious obeisance to the cited authors, especially to the travelling ones, both Germans and French, for the Philippine ethnography has greatly advanced although it has not arrived to its affected journey. Those learned authors with profundity of their studies about these races had not reached identical conclusions.

Despite their differences, all concurred in the racial ethnography of the Philippine archipelago. It showed that the Philippines had never been inhabited by a single group of people, specially in historical times.

On the arrival of the Spaniards, there were a great number of tribes who produced confusion in the scientific classifications and diverse denominations added perplexity. But Dr. Barrows said, "We have a superlative denominations of people that are practically identical".[43]

As F. Martinez de Zuniga said, "Indeed found two races those we know as Aetas or Negritos and Indios". This classification with minor difference was the one adopted by the majority of the authors.

The denomination of the Indios (as we have seen in advance) were applied by the Spaniards to all the Philippine inhabitants; it was ethnographically improper, like the one applied to the Malayan Mohamedans whom they called Moros.

---

[43] **Encyclopedia España**, Vol. 23, page 1356

All the authors seemed to have concurred that it was not in the origin that caused a multitude of arguments.

The groups of Aetas had been conserved, a difference with the second group that has been profoundly altered due to their inter-marriage with other races.

Montano, the French author, presented his Brief to the Public Ministry of Instruction on the ethnographical zones:

(a) The interior zone – the Negritos or Papua-Filipinos who were pushed by the Indonesians to the interior places.[44]

(b) Zone occupied by the Indonesians, who for a time were pushed by the Malayans.

(c) Zone exterior – the people along the coast were called Fili-pinos. These theories established the work and observation of Montano and other authors about the Oriental races. The cited au-thor added – "the Filipino race ought to be altered due to the con-tinuous immigrations of other races in the islands.

With respect to the Indonesians, their coming to the islands were not established by the ancient authors. The excavation findings we presented will settle the matter:[45] For the majority of the ethnogra-phers had the unanimity of not knowing where these peole ought to belong. Some said they belonged to the Battaks, others to the Malays. Spanish authors as well as Dr. Kern interpreted these races as Indostan or Indo.

(a) Negritos or Aetas

The name Negritos or Negrillos were given by the Spaniards; other names were – Aetas, Atis, Tas, Etas, Adtas, Abulons and Dumagats. These people were the first groups of Montano and were in the interior zone.

The Papua-Melanese[46] which extends from Melanesia, New Guinea and part of Micronesia and seemed to belong to the groups of the Adamaneses, the Semang of Malaca and the

---

[44] Haberlandt- Ethnography, page 192.
[45] Ibid. Map No.2 The Negritos should not be confused with the Papuans
[46] Ibid

The Igorrot Attire of Mountain Province

Negritos of the Philippines. In the confines of those areas, multiple of mixes were produced with the Austrassicans with Malay type (New Guinea).

The race was noted to be different from the Austrasicans who seemed to have established themselves in various capacities.[47]

The Negritos were the only ones found pure by the Spaniards, and still exist today. A nomad race, independent, who repulsed union and mixtures with others; they wasted their time or existence in general isolation at a risk of extinction. Thus, the race of the Aetas will weaken some day and will be reduced to complete extinction, defeated by robust invaders and of higher grade of culture.

It is the general opinion that the Aetas were the aborigines of the Philipine archipelago. They established themselves in the interior area, because of their intractable, nomadic and misanthropic character. Shunning mankind, they were banished to the thickness of the forest by the Malays and Indonesian invaders.

In the opinion of many authors, they were descendants of the Papua-Melanesians. Blumentritt said that they were the nephew, while Semper said that there were historical information about them. But ethnographers no less respectable refuted this. Mr. Thevenot assured that the great and special physique of the Negritos, indicated that they had no relation with those of New Guinea, Australia, New Caledonia and more of Africa.

Dr. Montano and Mr. Jordana said that these Aetas descended from the black race in the remote past, assuring that they resemble those Negritos. They said:

"The Negritos were barbaric people, foresters who lived on plants and mountain products. They were nude and covered their private parts with handkerchiefs they called bajaques taken from bark of trees and rattan; wore bracelets of various colors, wreaths on their heads, molds on their arms and feather of gauls."

They had no laws and government; no parentage and obeyed

---

[47] M. Haberlandt Ethnography, page 92.

the lineage of a family of their chief or their cabesa. They had no religion or if there was any, it was very nil. They were called Negritos by the Spaniards because they were black and had curly hair like the Ethiopians. There are still a lot of them living in the jungles of the Philippines.

In this same work it said: These Negritos were commonly believed to be the first inhabitants of the Philippine archipelago who came from Sumatra, Borneo, Java, Madagascar and other Occidental islands. If it were asked where this race came from, their answer will be from the interior of India, as they looked different from those of Africa and Ethiopia. They came from New Guinea which is nearer the Philippines.[48]

(b) Polynesians:

The Austrasican race, called Malay Polenesians before the arrival of the Spaniards, has been included in the modern ethnology because of the acknowledged linguistic connection with certain people of Indo-China: (the Monkomer people) the people of Indostan (Mandakol) the Polenesians, the Malenesians and the Oceanians. [49]

The great expansion of this race was notable or remarkable because it occupied one third of the maximum circle.[50]

This race was divided into two types:

(a) Indonesian type
(b) Polynesian type

The racial characteristic of the Indonesians: clear brown skin, black hair, undulatory voice. They were found in the interior islands comprising the Batacks, the Dayacs, the Igorots, the Formosans and Indo-Chinese, etc.

Among the archipelago Filipinos who corresponded to the second zone of Montano were the following different ethnic groups:

[48] F. Colin – opinion cited
[49] Ethnography – M. Haberlandt page 191 y s s. Ibid.
[50] Ibid 2 Map. It was expected from Madagascar up to the Islands of Pascua

    (I)   Tinguianes or Itanes
    (II) Igorrotes
  (III) Itetepanes
  (IV) Guiananes
   (V) Cadenes
  (VI) Calanas
 (VII) Apayaos
(VIII) Puaos
  (IX) Ibalaos or Ilongots
   (X) Burics
  (XI) Itais
 (XII) Riapis
(XIII) Andangs
(XIV) Ilayas

The Indonesians arrived first from the South of the continent of Asia in great waves of immigration in the first quarter of the millennium before our era.[51]

Their culture was more superior to the Negritos.

Among these numerous people are the following:

(1) *The Igorots*[52]

They formed a great group and occupied the wide range of the cordilleras of Pangasinan until Ituy, the oriental part of the same province, the capital of the valley of Agno in front of Namacpacan.

They were fleshy, fat and had big forms, short and dark brown. They were short with big black eyes and taller than the interior people; the cheeks well developed and wide. Their hair was smooth but straight, hard and shiny, that was noticeable.

(2) *The Ifugaos*[53]

They were brave and fierce, and seldom got down the mountains; the local force hurt their character and passive nature; their features were similar to the Japanese.

---

[51] Diccionario Estadistico Historico de las Islas Filipinas, p. 52.
[52] Ibid.
[53] Ibid

(3) *The Apayaos*

They lived in the mountains that divided the province of Cagayan and the Ilocos. They subsisted on rice and roots. They were distinguished from the other tribes particularly in the making of their houses, like the Tagalogs.

(4) *The Ibulaos and the Ilongots*

These tribes were reduced in numbers and occupied the mountains of Nueva Ecija and the Caraballo mountain of Baler. They were short and a little robust; they maintained their plundering lifestyle.

(5) *The Burics*

These groups differ a little from the Igorots being fleshy and vigorous; they occupied the mountains that are the prolongation of the province of Ilocos Sur till the top central chain mingling with the Igorots in the wide cordillera of Pangasinan . They are industrious and their customs humane.

(6) *The Malays*

They consider this race to belong to the Mongolian race with their black hair and yellow skin.[54] According to tradition, they came from Menangkabau, but their true country was to be found in Indonesia.

This curious hypothesis of their origin was given by Martinez de Zuniga which we expounded in continuation of what Mas had given.[55] This author wanted to demonstrate first the origin of the Malays of Borneo, where he said that the Malays were born from the white race mixed with the black race of New Guinea. He proved that there were connections between the languages of the Americas and the Malays, considering their geographical situation; that the wind blew towards that continent than to a contrary route. A modern traveler who had written a book about the Oceaneans belied the theory of the indicated religious but had not

[54] M. Haberlandt, Ethnografica, p 191
[55] Mas, Historia de Filipina, p 1 y ss

38

given the reasons and with a magistral tone said "it was a great error".

But it is sure to encounter in the idioms of the Americas and the Malays many terminations and analogous works which are sometimes exact.

Historical documents asserted that people from other Malay islands came to the Philippines in Barangay or Barangayan tribes with their chiefs or head. The word came from ancient Greece and referred to group of people with a chief or leader. Similarly Paroquia came from ancient Rome and also meant a group of people with a leader or chief. Barangay is used in rural areas while Paroquia is used in urban areas. Paroquia has been in continuous use in the Philippines where as Barangay is only used lately by the Philippine government, to expedite cases before it reaches higher courts.

Barangay or Barangayan, like the word Paroquia, meant a group of people led by a chief. In ancient Rome Paroquia was sometimes called Colleciones. Both terms refer to a form of government or public administration.

On the basis of language, Dr. P.A. Bareido demonstrated in his Doctoral Thesis the connection between the malay and the Philippine languages.[56]

From this stock, the Malays belong to the third zone of Montano; where the Philippine sub-races came and corresponded by the following groups:

(I) Tagalogs

(II) Visayans

(III) Pampangos

(IV) Pangasinanes

(V) Bicolanos

(VI) Ilocanos

---

[56] Ibid

These people were more cultured and numerous as had been described by many authors in the past.

As a final part of this chapter, we are clarifying the significance of some terms.

With respect to the word Indo, it expressed no technological filiation with the inhabitants of the Philippine archipelago.

The Spaniards used Indo as a common name for all the inhabitants of the Philippine archipelago. This is a well known error. This denomination should be repulsed for it only showed indifference, ridicule and injustice.

The name Indigena was very ambiguous and vague and neither determined the inhabitants.

With respect to the Tagalogs, the inhabitants of the Philippines are generally called so, including the Visayans, the Ilocanos the Pampangos, the Bicolanos, Pangasinan etc.

In a strict sense, this word is exclusively for the Tagalogs because they occupied the banks of rivers. Tagalog was composed of the terms taga and ilog, joined together it became tagailog, which meant people living on the banks of rivers. This confirmed the tradition of Father Collins. The Malays came from the river banks in the middle of Sumatra, passing through Borneo.

Malayans dominated all inhabitants who came from the Malay coasts of Borneo near Malaca, where they found a Malaca community; in Tagalog malayo signifies far.

The following is a complete frame of the Filipino ethnic group's descriptions:

(a) NEGRITOS

Thigh	Elegant
Skin	Coffee colored and toasted
Body	Straight and light
Hair	Very black and a little kinky
Head	Round and small

Front	Straight
Eyes	Bigger than the eyes of the Malays
Eyebrow	A little arched
Eyelash	Long
Mouth	Medium or small and flat
Lips	Medium
Teeth	Long and Strong
Upper jaw	Natural
Lower jaw	Well formed
Breast	Straight but supple
Body's position	Smart and free
Hips	Well developed and strong
Legs	Thin
Feet	Small
Flesh	Hard

(b) <u>MALAYS</u> (pure Indos)

Height	Elegant, medium and sometime tall
Skin	Copper colored and smooth
Body	Generally slim and well formed
Hair	Black, straight, thick and knotty
Head	Medium round, flat on the back
Eyes	Brilliant
Front	Straight and sometimes uncovered
Eyebrow	Thick and arched
Eyelashes	Long
Nose	Medium but generally flat
Mouth	Generally corpulent
Lips	Medium
Teeth	White, well lined and Strong

Upper Jaw	Natural
Lower Jaw	Regular and strong
Breast	Long, hard and straight among women
Position of body	Elegant and gracious
Hips	Well developed and hard
Thigh	Thin
Legs	Slender
Feet	Small
Flesh	Hard
Hair	Lightly wooly

This chart was taken from the work of Buceta and Bravo, pp 57 and ss.

THE LANGUAGE

A. INTRODUCTION

The crucial tenet of our work is: Were our forefathers civilized upon the arrival of the Spaniards in the Philippines ? Language provides the answer. As historians have said, language is the key to understanding and underscores the pre-development of nations.

This chapter introduces what linguists call **language** and certain terms such as **dialects** and **idioms.**

For a better understanding of the psychological intricacies of language, we present it in detailed form so that all Filipinos, including the men on the street, will embrace it, thus satisfying their curiosity and clarifying any misunderstanding.

We define the difference between dialect and idioms to avoid controversies on dogmatic contents. Other authors could have other ideas but without our definition we would lack the ability to explain.

What is language? First we have to distinguish its extent and exact or accurate sense. In its extensive term it may mean a mode of expression of an internal reality. In this sense we talk of the language of animals, plant, etc. As we will see later, language is exclusively the patrimony of man being rational.

"Stricto sensu", consider and follow what Menendes Pidal said, "It is a system of signs which are principally sonorous, that serves to manifest our physical world". Language is not conjunctive but a system of organization and instrument to the creation of the human activity that is secular once in a century and is constant.

In terms of classification we cite the common divisions: spoken language, written, mimic or signs:

Bulls gave the following:

1. Expression: It gives a manifestation of our state. It is therefore a system.

2. An appeal or call: When we see someone fleeing from a fire, we assume that someone is calling for help from others. It is linguistic in this sense and therefore is a sign.

These classes of signs exist among animals but the language that is appropriately human possesses a representative function.

3. Representation Table is a precisely representative idea and is a historical one. Table consists of four signs and is a symbol of an object.

Language and its elements are social products that are imposed on an individual. Language is like the dress code and style imposed by social convention.

The word language is from the Latin word "lingua" whose etymological word formation expresses the organ that employs the articulation of the distinct pronunciation of the first word and syllables.

Dialect is a regional variety of a language distinguished by pronunciation, grammar or vocabulary.[57]

Idioms is an expression of a given language peculiar to a group of people.

Language and idioms are synonymous terms and are included in the system of linguistic signs.

According to Mas-Muller, the term language ought to refer to a system of linguistic system or signs which are fixed and retained in its linguistic evolution as in the case in Rome, Israel, Greece, etc.

Idioms are artificial forms of language, while dialects are forms manifesting natural life.

In our reference to the Filipino language, we employ the term language to the Tagalogs, Visayas and Ilocanos and to other dialects which have the same roots.

With this definition, we conclude that Language is a typical human activity for rationals and with characteristic difference

---

[57] American Heritage Dictionary

among irrationals. This does not mean that outside the human race, there is no medium to express sensation, either in instinctive or communicative expression.[58]

These arguments strongly supported the Mexican council which condemned the thesis sustained by some authors that the ancient Filipinos were irrational and looked seemingly like monkeys[59].

At the threshold of uncertainty authors confidently envisioned that language stands forth in the country's civilization and development and that language is the wealth of all nations and all beings.

Abel Remusat, a celebrated Orientalist said, that the "language of a nation is the complete and most faithful mirror of its civilization, a complete frame of the social revolution that has marked its existence". To that thought Garcia Ayosu added, "The dominating opinion of a nation is manifested in Language".

The perfection of the alphabet was found to be in direct relation to the scientific and cultural progress of a nation, in its lexicography and syntax, where it manifests desires, aesthetic sentiments and the intellectual power of the human race.

If this is true in respect to grammar, likewise vocabulary is the authentic testimony to the imaginative power of the people, their progress about the knowledge of nature and influence on other existing relations.

Language has a tremendous impact on the lives and souls of every nation. It crosses the barriers of geography, culture, and

---

[58] In this sense actions and modulation of the voice in the manner of interjections manifest sensitive state of expression like fear, anger, pain and contentment. Examples of these are the sounds made by monkeys, rabbit, dogs, etc. among the domesticated animals the dogs congeries were like those of human. They know multiple differences of communicative expressions, as given in the examples of L. Geiger

[59] Father Delgado in reference to their opinion judged them with the following... "To me these authors were of critical and of unmelancholic temper. I supposed and believed that these authors did not deny this nor differentiated the man Indio, but only their natural actions and inclinations". Opinion cited, p 287.

politics and thus emerges as a beacon light of understanding. It has a tremendous impact on families and communities of nations.[60]

Language has to be in every field of action. It is the interpreter of culture and civilization of the day. The details in language history are all but infinite in variety and extent reflecting the inquisitiveness and acumen of people.

It is obvious that language is so universally inherent in all changes in political and economic status thus enhancing the growth of nations.[61]

There is probably no language in which all the words are formed through its own process from the original root.[62] Much persistence has been devoted to tracing of some thousand lone words from more or less remote languages that have heretofore left without etymology or ascribed vaguely to "native sources".[63]

The use of idioms is a cultural manifestation in itself and is a vehicle of civilization. For this reason it expresses the advance development of people. In Idioms alone, we have the consistency to confirm in this chapter that language enhanced the intense, cultural development of the Filipino people who were actually civilized prior to the arrival of the Spaniards in our shores. So Father Juan dela Costa said, "how could we confirm and understand a nation called irrational when men and women knew how to read and write?"[64]

---

[60] International Webster Dictionary, referring to history.

[61] Ibid.

[62] Cited by Enrique d' Almonte in his work about the formation and evolution of the sob-razas Indonesia and Malaysia, p. 127

[63] Agustin Barreiro, p. 26

[64] (1) The strength and beauty of our language was cited by W. Retana **Bibliografico** Chapter XVII. **Las Letras de Filipinas** p. 52 where it said, *"The islanders were inclined to read and write, that there was no one either man nor woman who could not read and write the proper letters of the islands in Manila which were different from those of India, Japan and China."*

The first who brougth this to light was Father Collin in his book, **Labor Evangelica**, p. 57, where he said, referring to the Tagalogs, *"They wrote in big and delicate signature and courtesies...."* It was also cited by Morga in his book, **Sucessos**, Vol. 40

Paterno also cited this in his book, **La Antigua Civilization Tagala**, p. 368, where he said *"They wrote not in syllables or symbols but in a language that was courteous, impressive, artful and elegant for it had the quality of the four best languages of the world. Greeks, Hebrew, Spanish and Latin".*

Undoubtedly this point of view referred to the Tagalogs. Nonetheless many authors did not see the difference between the Aetas and the Tagalogs that unfairly mistook one for the whole.

These revealed manifestations by several ancient authors were deeply entrenched and remained as the pillars of our Filipino culture. Not knowing whence and how, it must have been a miracle of "gossalalia," which were words that were coined centuries ago to denote the practice of the charismatic speaking in a language that was not readily understood by speakers of any of the known languages."

It could not be a misgotten mission, so no one should be bewildered when we say that from the jungles of the East, the mighty civilization of Egypt, Greece and Rome had reached the Philippine shores. This we believed was not a forced exodus, but an apparent plan from Divine Providence, which we will unravel in the rest of our chapters.

Europe itself is in Asia, made up of small peninsulas. Its relative small continents contain many striking contrasts paralleled by the diversity of people and cultures which once included the great ancient Greek culture and the Roman civilization. The maritime outlook in the Western areas of Europe led to the great exploration that took these people and their culture to the furthest corners of the Earth.[65]

No doubt the above event or fact has a far-reaching effect on our culture, where authors of antiquity described the seemingly supernatural phenomenon of our ancient culture, that either any human law or natures law can support the contention which we had gone a long way proving it.

There were other occasions for fundamental truths, but the value of psychological studies were underestimated and brushed aside. Few were willing to accept nor ponder its depth.

Amidst all the spectacular elements of language, it had a decisive base in the ancient ethnography. As observed by H.

---

[65] The Great World Atlas page 96.

Haberlandt,[66] "Language cannot serve as a general base of a perfect classification that could be converted or changed; that could reflect the true parentage or connections of people. Many idioms showed among them various grades without being sure of the parentage of the people. In many cases the different linguistic parentage that favor grammatical structure in the vocabulary or in formal elements served as linguistic elements that did not always coincide in the division of races; although according to anthropologists they sometime concurred."

B. PRE-SPANISH LANGUAGE OF THE PHILIPPINES

Unlike other fields of learning, language, like history, is boundless in many ways. We can get the clearest, most encompassing of what a culture, a society, an individual or a nation has gone through by looking at the past of their enduring legacy, specially language.

From a conceptual viewpoint, language is intimately linked to the advancement and development of nations. Herewith we present conjunctive realities of the Philippine language before the arrival of the Spaniards in the islands. We confirmed with satisfaction the great number of works written by the Spanish missionaries, with a counter view on the other works which had considerably facilitated our research in basic element that were indispensable to our work. We continually reviewed our studies and conclusion with the modern philology.

We divided this epigraph into five fundamental components in order to get a clear overview of its content:

(a) Classification

Like ethnography the Philippine language had many things that can be considered astounding. There were peculiar profusion of diverse elements.

If language is to be understood, we have what Mas said, "Every dialect that is similar with the rest, the Philippines had a hundred

---

[66] H. Haberlandt, **Etnografia**, p. 196 y ss. vv

dialects, but all of them were corruptions, or variations of a form which is part of one family known by Etnographers as Malay." This did not mean that we will not have occasion to deny or confirm it.

The circumstantial geographic situation and political bearing failed to impose the individual's dialect on his neighbor to serve as a basis for the establishment of a common language, as what happened to the people of Europe. Other factors were the lack of communication due to distance and the continuous antagonism among the different tribes. All these had considerable factor that facilitated the paulitanian disintegration of the original language and its multiplication. Neighborhood integration was not possible due to its 'geographical situation where numerous islands in the same land kept them away from each other. It was a natural isolation which produced political and cultural autonomy that without commercial relation to counter it, there would be no potential significance of one language. Added to these were the waves of immigration from other countries.

If the isolation of the different islands within the Philippines had caused an impasse to the language, nevertheless, it was countered by the immigration of people from other countries. Its uncloistered position, natural beauty and wealth together with its friendly inhabitants were attractions for the adventurous immigrants from other shores.

Thus the main strength and beauty of the Philippine language was the diversity of people who influenced it.

The above takes into account what ancient authors had said "The Philippines is not a single race but a conglomeration of different ethnic groups or races."

To this we concur and we hope cynics will not underestimate this fact.

Upon the arrival of the Spaniards there were various dialects even in the island of Luzon. The Tagalog and Visayan dialects were considered the mother language of the archipelago. The Tagalog dialect was the most spoken in the provinces of Tondo, Bulacan, Batangas, Laguna, Tayabas, Cavite, Mindoro, Zamboanga and also in the islands of the Marianas where the deportees were taken.

The Visayan language was spoken in all the Visayan islands although there were some differences in some provinces; hence, the people from Samar could not understand the Ilongos, although they were related.

The following citations show the dialects and sub-dialects:

1. Ilongo was spoken in the islands of Panay, Romblon, Tablas, Cebuyan in the northwest part of Negros, Zamboanga, Misamis and Caraga.

2. Capiz differed a little bit from that of Iloilo.

3. Cebuano, considered a particular language, was spoken in the islands of Bohol and part of Negros, all of Cebu. The natives easily understood Ilongo.

4. The people from the islands of Camarines and Paragua (Palawan) spoke a mixture of the Tagalog and Visayan language.

The islands of Mindanao, similar to the island of Luzon were divided in a great number of tribes, each with a particular dialect. **The various tribes and dialects were too numerous to detail. However, the dialect spoken was generally Illan, one similar to the Malayan.**

In Luzon, the Tingians, Igorots, Ifugaos, Ibilaos, etc. spoke various tribal dialects.

(b) Origin

Buceta set the tone when he said, "Many had worked in the investigation of the origin of the language of the Philippine archipelago and its relation with the antique languages. They figured that the Philippine language came from the Sanskrit; others found sparks from the Chinese and Japanese and a few from the Hebrew language. Others speculated that it was an original language. Intrigued by the variety of suppositions, we had these occasions to confirm in the chapter that their arguments were weak. We had a clear idea that the real connections were influences performed by the cited languages and in no way descended from them.

Language is deeply rooted in the history of all nations.

"The extreme Orient had a particular progeny of languages including that of the Hebrew,... as a result of the changes produced by topical action belonging to a place and culture and the delay in time of other nations," continued Buceta.

It was originally believed that the Philippine dialects ought to have their origin from the Malays, which was primeval or original.

Isabelo delos Reyes said that Buceta was almost right because this Malay language was a primitive one which was derived from primitive Sanskrit believed to be dead or extinct. Nevertheless, many ancient authors said that they encountered in this idiom the principle and form of the language of Slava, Latin, Greek, etc.

Through analysis we examined the cause, effect and manifestation in the principle of the conformity of the human race. Many authors still had qualms about the conformities of the human race.[67]

Errors often occur when alluded facts were not given adequate time for study and development. In point of record about the Philippine language, Jacquet and Blumentritt were also of the opinion that the Malay language was the mother tongue of the Philippine language.[68]

Like the Malay language, the Filipino language has no masculine or feminine gender. All nouns are in the common gender. To distinguish the numbers, another noun is added to the endings, or the first syllable is repeated[69]. Thus, the noun for "man" - *tao* - is

---

[67] Father Agustin Barreiro, an author who studied this subject, said, "Rigorously united with the Philippine idioms were grammatical procedures as well as the identify of terms usually used. There could be no doubt that there were some Malay and Polynesian idioms received from the same family who belonged to the polynesian of the Indian Archipelago north of Formosa, west of Madagascar, the eastern part of the multitude of islands which extended to New Zealand in the southern hemisphere."

[68] Isabelo delos Reyes, **Historia de los Ilocos**.

[69] Two procedures determined the filiation of languages. One was the old procedure of vocabulary comparison which had been the cause of lamentable errors. The other was the scientific procedure of establishing the parentage of language by comparing its grammatical forms. Our method mixed the two procedures.

singular and becomes *mga tao* in plural in the Tagalog dialect; In Ilocano, it is *tat tao*. Heart is *puso* and its plural form in Tagalog is *mga puso*. In Ilocano it is *pus puso*.

Generally the similarities in grammar and the vocabularies were great as seen in paragraphs dedicated to the descriptions. There should be no doubt from what influence the Philippine dialect or language descended directly or indirectly.[70]

Another phenomenon in the diversity of the Philippine language was the possibility that many immigrants came from the different provinces and the positions of the islands in its geographical locations as previously discussed.

Certain doubts existed on the origin of the dialects of the Igorots specially those of the Aetas.

According to the author, Paterno, the Igorots used many articulations, such as *ch*, a very interesting case considering that civilized people did not know that pronunciation. From here Galvey and many others inferred that this idiom was partly Chinese. Thus, instead of *dua* they pronounced it *chua* and in this way they formed words with many consonants. Their enumeration and manner of speaking sounded like the Philippine language. They understood their neighbors easily. From this it was believed that these native people spoke a language the essence of which was based on Philippine voice. However, majority of their language had a possible Chinese influence.

Our major research on the twilight of our ancient history was done in the rare section of the National Library of Madrid, Spain, where histories of old civilizations of the world were mostly found. Many people of different nationalities gravitated to this hall to research old civilizations.

---

[70] Father Collin in his Labor Evangelica said that the Philippine language descended from the Malay language and for its proof he made the following comparison

Spanish	Malay	Tagalog	Pampango	Visayan
cielo	languit	langit	banoa	langit
sol	mataari	arao	aldao	atlao
luna	bulan	buan	buluan	bulan

(c) Influence Received:

It looked very promising but we had a drawback from the different viewpoints of many authors. A deep interest in language and culture, the delicate interplay between literacy and civilization, sprung within us.

As indicated in our previous chapters the Philippine language experienced many influences from other languages either directly or indirectly.

Language is an open field. Various elements filter through it specially where there have been interaction caused by natural mediums which are combinations of circumstances, geographical situations, life's necessities and adventures.

It would be hard to envision why an interesting relation between the Philippines and the South American languages existed, such as Hebrew, and others who claimed that the Philippines had the same source as that of the origin of the Vasquence dialects.

Drawn together were the doubtful similarities and sometimes coincidences that gave the manifestations of the linguistic languages' parentage and not its filiations. We limit ourselves to describing some examples of notable influences admitted by some authors.

The interesting connections of these South American and Philippine languages were observed by Father Martinez de Zuniga. His assertions were censured by many authors [71] but has not given any demonstration to contradict such relations with the South American language.

As observed by Father Martinez de Zuniga, language connection existed between the Philippine language and South American language.[72] In his book, **History of the Philippines,** he "found a dictionary of only five terms which the Spaniards learned in this patagonian coast. One of these was the word *"balay"* that

---

[71] Paterno, **La Civilization Tagala,** p. 139
[72] Isabelo de los Reyes, **Historia de los Ilocos,** p. 81.

signified house also used as such by the Pampangos and Visayans; this could be an accident for there was no proof that the language of one was the language of the other. But in the wake of the South American nouns sounding like Philippine nouns, I procured a dictionary and failing to find one, I examined with care some terms in the language of Chile, which Arcilla brought in his Araucana. There I found many similarities of words with the Tagalog language." For example:

"The nouns in Chile is not foreign with the idioms of this language where the crow is called *cachili*, a pronoun given by the Malays to the sons of kings. Chilian is a town in Chile, and is a Tagalog composition where an 'a' may designate a place".

"Thus from *cachile* came *cachilian*, a place where marine crows were found. Another Tagalog composition was the place where the city of Santiago was found. From *"poquot"* came the word *"mapoquiot"* which was a place where these herbs grew in abundance.

In Chile the reduplication of the terms *itita, biobio, lemolemo,* etc. was also done by the Tagalog as in *atata, bilobilo, malalim-lamim, mataastaas, magandaganda,* etc. There is so much similarity in these Tagalog terms.

Actually it could be considered an accident if very few similar words were found in these two languages. Modern philologists were not agreeable to the method that was employed by Zuniga as they said it had no fundamental base.

A base that was sure and complete an investigation countenanced the relations between the Sanskrit and those languages.

Among the alien words that figured in the Tagalog language (that was the model of the rest), the most numerous were derived from the Sanskrit according to T.H. Tavera.[73] Upon learning the derivation of the principal language of Central Luzon, not few linguists believed that this language was derived from the language of India.

---

[73] El Sansctito en la Lengua Tagala. p. 5.

The Webster Dictionary in Reference to History recorded that the Sanskrit ceased being used during the third century before Christ and was succeeded by Parkrit which was intermixed with the language of Indonesia and the Arabs used in their religious books. Thus Sanskrit words were introduced in the Philippines by the Arabs and Persians during their brief stay in our land.

Historical records showed that Sanskrit was a source of the Philippine language as well as other Indo-European languages, but its product could not have its name, as investigated by many ancient authors. It had just enriched the Philippine language for the complexities necessary for a new life that was brought by colonization. This resulted in the convenience and usefulness in commerce and industry. Luckily it did not erase or obscure the national idioms but left only some residue that were still considered doubtful by many ancient authors.

The Sanskrit had no monument of its own but its forms and roots were made out to a large extent by scientific comparison from the language that descended from it.[74]

Generally civilized or enlightened idioms hardly suffered modification as could be observed in many Latin words.[75]

Thus the number of Sanskrit and Malay words that found their way in the Philippine language were not numerous to be called Sanskrit or Malay; some of which were not of popular currency. We also found no evidence that Malays sought to perpetuate or extend the use of their language except in some regions of Mindanao where Mohammedanism was practiced.

Through relentless efforts we uncovered many errors; nevertheless, they had enriched our idioms by supplying the deficiency of some of our words.

(d) Description of Common Characters:

From its words of sufficient importance of the etymology of the

---

[74] New Webster Dictionary Reference to History.
[75] R. Menendes Pidal, Manual De Gramatica Española, Madrid 1952, p.10

word presented, we attempted to show the development of the form and meaning within the language, the source and how it came to the Philippine language and its derivation and relationship.

The common word to denote place among the Persians and the Arabs was to add *an* to the endings of the words, as in *languis* (oil), which becomes *languisan*. In Tagalog, Persian and Arabic *candle-shema* became *shemadan* which meant candlestick; Indus, Indio, Industan – the country of the Indios[76] Chile-chilian, poqiout - mapoqiout.

Regarding the relation of the Philippine language with others, Father Cipriano Arcilla referred it to the monumental **Catalogo de las Languajes** of Hervas Tanduru which was considered the first to establish the linguistic comparison of the Philippines; before the book of the Franciscan Father Cyanguran where his **Tagalismo Elucidad** (Mexico, 1742), compared the Tagalog with that of the Chinese, the Greeks and Hebrews.

In consonance with the time, the Chinese had not only ten words in the Philippine language. Recorded in the International Webster dictionary there were one hundred words in the English language inspite of the distance and their much later contacts with the Chinese.

Of particular interest it would not be superfluous to discern the piety of the Filipinos that could be an influence of Confucianism whose cardinal virtues were piety, education, statesmanship and religiousness. The Chinese were among the first who came to the Philippines when the earth's ice cap receded, now known as the South China sea.[77]

In view of the Hindu influence the Philippine literature had taken new forms and acquired vigor under the influence of the Hindus. The poets learned verses in consonants. In general those who knew more of this Philippine language, sustained an evolution of the Javanese language due to the alluded circumstances though it was of moderate scale.

---

[76] Cipriano Marcilla, Los Antiguos alfabetos, p.1.
[77] David Howard Bain, sitting in Darkness, p. 109.

According to Pardo de Tavera the Hindus did not only transact simple commerce in the archipelago, but also dominated various fields specially in places where their dialects could be used more like in the regions of the Tagalogs, the Visayans, the Ilocanos and the Pampangos. This was due to the linguistic influence. The words adopted expressed names of dignity or ranks, high fucntionaries, nobles, names of arms and fortitude, etc.

We could cite many examples of the Sanskrit influence on the more advanced dialects of the archipelago and in order not to tire the reader, we will only give a few examples of Sanskrit influence enumerated by T.H. Pardo de Tavera and Kern Burouf[78] to the Tagalog dialects and that of Isabelo de los Reyes to the dialects of the Ilocanos. Parts of the examples given are as follows:

Aga in Sanskrit signified sun. In the Malay dialect it signified elevation and glorification. In the Tagalog dialect it meant sunrise or morning. In Sanskrit *hantu* was also *hantu*. In Malay it signified spirit, phantom, bad temper. Among the Tagalogs it meant the image of the dead and eventually became *anito*.

The disappearance of the initial 'f' in the Tagalog and Pampango dialects was due to the direct introduction of Javanese instead of the Sanskrit.

The authors also showed that many Arab and Persian terms were in conformity with that of the Malay language. But these Sanskrit-Malay terms had given very few terms to the Philippine language and with the arrival of the Spaniards their influence ended.

In the study of the Philippine language it had shown a great flexibility in the assimilation of words of foreign languages, yet it had not allowed other nations to eradicate, deaden or place it under siege like some South American languages that gradually disappeared. Like the Spanish language had enriched its vocabulary throughout the ages. The Chinese, frequent visitors to the archipelago, were the first in contact with the Filipinos. But somewhat poignantly viewed, its influence was underestimated.

---

[78] T.H. Pardo de Tavera based his opinion on combination of Sanskrit words.

This was Father Martinez de Zuniga description of the Chinese influence on the Philippine language: hardly could we find ten words despite its frequent and long relations with the Filipino people. Therefore a detailed description should be provided principally about social and religious morals which were very much overlooked. He said that it was but natural that the Filipinos learned only words for names of food, kitchen utensils and some shipping but had nothing to do with words about intellectual acts that signified moral, religion, political and institutions of social life. The Chinese came simply to buy, sell and negotiate. They never preoccupied themselves to propagate religion for fear that other races would imitate and take advantage of what their country exclusively had.

"That China sent only ignorant, adventurous and low class people of the coast... that these people sail out of the coasts with the single purpose to go to a land where they could make a fortune. Thus, the Philippines was never given an education by the Chinese."*

If records showed that ten Chinese words could hardly be found in our Philippine language, then we believe that the interest on the age of things, tradition, culture and education had reached the Philippines on those unrecorded times.

The strong sensibilities of humanitarian aspect in social and family behavior which extended to friends and foreigners had no source and background but sounds exactly like Chinese words:

(a) *Ate* for the eldest sister (a sign of respect)

(b) *Siajo* for brother-in-law (a sign of respect)

(c) *Inso* for sister-in-law (a sign of respect)

(d) *Cuya* for oldest brother (a sign of respect)

The words below were used as prefixes for the second eldest sisters or brothers:

---

* C. Marcilla, **Los Antiguos Alfabetos de Filipinas.**, p. 1

(a) *Ate* Maria

(b) *Cuya* Pedro

(c) *Siajo* Simon

(d) *Inso* Maria

Uncles and aunts were called <u>*"Caca"*</u>, denoting sign of respect.

Persons without affinity were called with the prefix <u>ale</u> for women and <u>mama</u> for men. Without these prefixes it would be a sign of bad manners and ill family training. These were essential elements in the Filipino tradition.

Major research showed that upon the arrival of the Spaniards in the Philippines, now affectionately called "Pearl of the Oriental Seas", they found a unique culture and Christian-like civilization. They saw that the transition of the inhabitants from the primitive stage to urbanity had long time passed, made undoubtedly possible by the unbroken legacy of commitments to moral values and in depth discipline to learn what we are today. The unbroken legacies were potential elements inherent to mankind endowed by "Mother Nature" to mark the relation between man and God. There should be no qualms to call this feat education which is synonymous to civilization. In this vein there could be no monopoly of education and culture of nations.

These educational feats generated in us a view that there were schools of learning in some fashion where men and women could have been taught thereby ushering in a new era called civilization.

As it is possible to tell the weather by certain signs, one should pay attention and accept reality. The ancient authors saw the signs of the civilized state of our forefathers and thus, in their anecdotal accounts, pictured our ancient social and economic developments. A place of learning crafts was described. Their lasting achievements were stamped in our tradition and received wide acclaim by many authors.

People enjoying such degree of development herein mentioned cannot be born out of imagination of young men and women who had never been outside the community. It has been shown in early history that young people did not acquire knowledge unless they had economic reason to do so. Unless taught in organized school, the measure would not be an authenticated one or a standardized activity.

Experience had shown that people acquired knowledge of letters in schools; otherwise they would have lapsed back to illiteracy, specially if they did not put it into practice in their daily lives.

The Spaniards saw beauty and abundance in infinite details in the Filipino handiwork. The analytic descriptions of the peace and order together with the contentment of our ancient forebears reflected a reference to organized schools in technical fields equivalent to what we have today, although comparatively speaking our ancient schools were inferior to those existing today inasmuch as the center of our contemporary learning did not exist during those early days.

The histographer Jose Suncuya, after a laborious research, pieced out some bits of information about the educational system of the ancient Filipinos in his **Historia Pre-Spanica de las Islas de Panay** where he asserted that formalized education was known to the Filipinos during those times. He said there were schools which taught reading, writing and fencing for self-defense.[79]

It is obvious that our ancient history was unknown so we delved through the records the essential elements of education of our ancient people, what it had been, what it was about, what it was worth, its purpose to human society in its needs and aspirations and, above all, the character and direction of its civilization. With all these essential elements we found that they had shared ideals and wisdom to be a rightful member of the global community of nations though in the past they were behind the scenes. They had the character and direction to civilization which amazed many authors who pictured them as the gem of the Oriental seas.

(e) The Philippine Alphabet

---

[79] Manila Bulletin.

The Philippines had their system of writing before the arrival of the Spaniards.

From our research we formed the impression that many authors, both ancient and modern, have woven historical adventures depicting minute details of our ancient forefathers. These were entangled with some contradictions, inconsistencies and illogical explanations. We could have abandoned this if it were not for the gist of 19th century essayist, Thomas Carlyle, who said "Every noble work seems impossible at first, but if truth exists, it can be done and demonstrated in many ways, if research is sufficient in depth, both in efforts, sincerity and patience."

The authors had contradictory opinions about the alphabet of our ancient people.[80] However, in the honor of truth we yield to the authority of the Spanish chroniclers on the subject.

What we contest is the dependence on the primary knowledge in the classification and characteristic of the Filipino alphabet. What we maintain is that there is only one Filipino alphabet and it had Malay influence due to the posterior modification of the Sanskrit as we will discuss later.

The first Filipino alphabet became known in Europe through the work of the Spanish Jesuit. The question of its primary publication came from the narration given by F. Chirino in his book **Relacion de las Islas Filipinas,** edited in Rome in 1604.[81]

The problem that has not been settled was the direction of the written alphabet which produced major controversies among the ancient and modern authors. The ancient authors who opposed their opinions were Chirino, Santa Ines and San Antonio; the modern ones were Mas, Jacquet and Isabel de los Reyes. This question, as we have said, is not relevant to our work.

The entirety of the words used in their writing constituted the alphabets called *baybayin*. The word *baybayin* according to

---

[80] Retana, Apartado Bibliographo, Vol. II, p. 180 y ss

[81] Int. Dictionary in Reference to History Father Chirino's illustration of our alphabet was not unique as the letters looked like the letters of the Eastern alphabets such as those of the Chinese and the Hebrews.

Paterno came from *babai* or *babae* which signified the female genital organ. The corresponding character of the Latin letter "I" was a sign of the *lalake*, a design or figure of the male sexual organ. The female and male signs untied together symbolized light and formed the name of *Bathala*, or the Almighty, Creator of all.

These figures, together with the lines emitted by the rays of the sun in the sky, were believed to have formed the Tagalog characters and other dialects, making the sounds of "ba" as the root of the dialects. Many authors considered the various terms as independent from other dialect.

The records of many authors on the Filipino consonants and vowels are not complete. Before the arrival of the Spaniards the alphabet contained 16 letters which were similar to the corresponding letters of the ancient alphabets of the world – Phoenicians, Celts, Spanish, Greeks and Latins.

The vowels were: a, e, i, o, u.

The first vowel corresponded to the Latin letter a, It was full and sonorous. The others were guttural short a and others were long a, slightly guttural and full.

The second vowel corresponded to the vowels e, i, had a sound between the light pronunciation of the two Latin characters but not exactly the *e* or the *i*.

The third vowel is represented by o or u of the Latin alphabet and was a specie of a dipthong of the Latin alphabet.

All consonants were pronounced with the sound of the first vowel a.

To express the sound of vowel e to the sound of vowel i a point is placed below e.

A point below vowel o will get vowel u.

Examples – ba becomes be or bi, the last consonant of the syllable is suppressed.

These especialties of the Philippine alphabets were observe by the missionaries. These feats showed that even before the time of Christ our ancient people were abreast with the style of the world's writing. Father Chirino took the picture of our alphabet's Manuscript.

The use of the alphabet on strictly phonetic bases seemed to have been due to the Semitic people of the early part of the second millennium before Christ who left a few inscriptions found and deciphered in the Sinai Peninsula.[82]

Ancient author's supposition that the self-made alphabet of our forefathers was purely Sanskrit must be discarded.

Unlike the Sanskrit our consonants were not usually pronounced as they were suppressed by the sound of the vowel as demonstrated in the graph of the alphabet of Father Chirino.

Amazingly the ingenuity of our ancient people were interpretative and creative. The formation of the baybayin was a phenomenon, similar to the abedecedario or a b c.

Father Chirino's illustration of our alphabet was not unique as the letters of the Eastern alphabets such as those of the Chinese and the Hebrews.

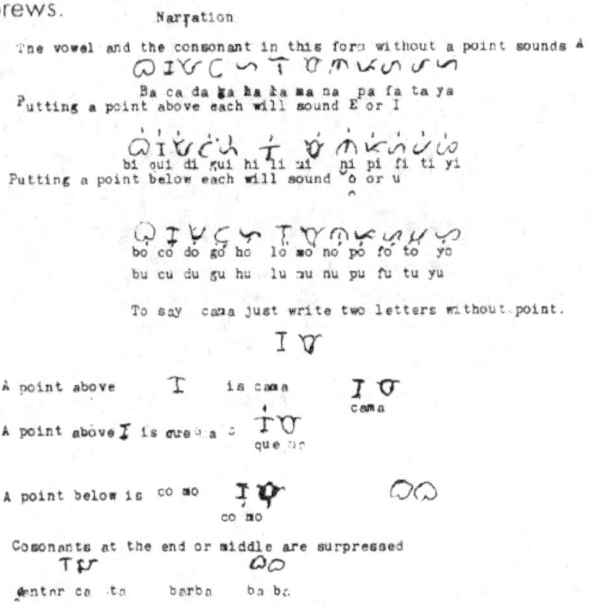

[82] As F. Marcilla said in his book **"The Ancient Philippine Alphabet:"** No one can deny the unfading glory of our religious compatriots who before others had settled the value of the language, with its grammatical rules and stamping the peculiarities of writing the ancient Filipino alphabet.

sentarse a esperar, que le pregunten lo que quiere; porque es mala crianza, dezir nada hasta ser preguntado. Mas la mayor criança está en el dezir, por que nunca le hablan de tu, ni en segunda persona de singular, ni de plurar. Sino siempre en la tercera. El señor; El principal, querra esto, o esto. De que aun enla Sagrada escritura, i lengua santa; i particularmente en los Salmos se hallan muchos exemplos. Particularmente ombre con muger; i muger con ombre; i muger con muger, aynque sean mui iguales, i de mediana suerte; nunca se tratan menos que Señor mio, Señora mia: i esto tras cada primera palabra. Viniendo yo Señor mio el Rio arriba. Vi señor mio, &c. El qual termino, i pronombre se sabe quan agradable, i amoroso sea, aun en las linguas demas importancia, quales son las tres mas sagradas Hebrea, Griega, i Latina. En tratos de cortesanias, i aficiones son estremados: i usan mucho el escrevirse con grandissimas, i delicadissimas finezas, i primores. En consequencia de lo qual usan mucho, el darse musicas. I aunque la Viguela, que llaman Cutyapi; no es mui artificiosa, ni la musica mui subida: no dexa de ser agra dable, i a ellos muche. Toncanla con una biveza, i destreza, que a quatro cuerdas, que tiene de alambre, las hazen hablar. Tenemos alla por cosa mui averiguada, que con solo el tocarlas, callando la boca, se dizen, i entienden todo lo que quieren i Cosa que no se sabe de otra ninguna nacion. Los Bissayas son mas rusticos, i llanos; como su lengua mas brozca, i grossera. No tienen tantos terminos de criança; como ni tenian letras: pues las tomaron de los Tagalos bien pocos años a. De las quales sera justo dezir alguna cosa: ya que emos dicho de las lenguas.

De las Letras de los Filipinas. Cap. XVII.

SOn tan dados todos estos Isleños al escrevir, i leer; que no ai casi ombre, i mucho menos muger; que no lea, i escriva en letras propias de la Isla de Manila, diversissimas de las de la China, i Iapon, i de la India: Como se vera de su Alfabeto, que es este.

Las vocales son tres: mas sirvenles de cinco; que son.

a	e i	o u

Las consonantes no son mas que doze: i sirven en el escrivir de

con-

confonante, i vocal , en efta forma . La letra fola, fin punto arriba,
ni a baxo ; fuena con A .

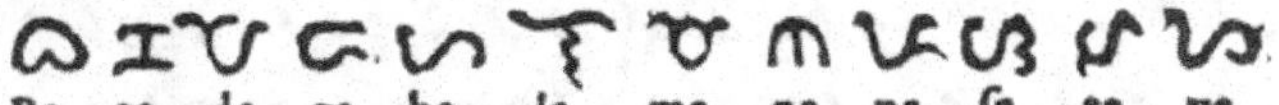

Ba ca da ga ha la ma na pa fa ta ya

Poniendo el puntillo arriba; fuena cada una deftas con E, o con I,

bi qui di gui hi li mi ni pi fi ti yi
be que de gue he le me ne pe fe te ye

Poniendo el puntillo abaxo ; fuena con O, o con u .

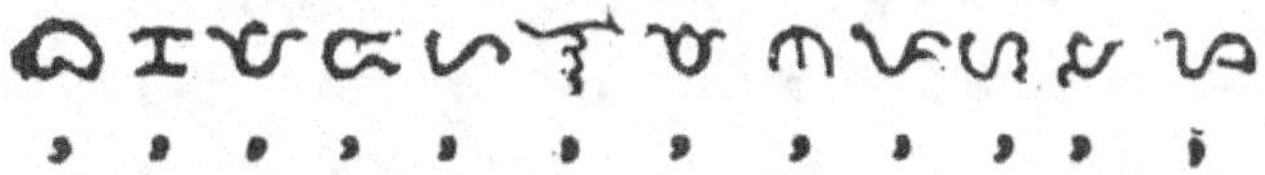

bo co do go ho lo mo no po fo to yo
bu cu du gu hu lu mu nu pu fu tu yu

Por manera que para dezir, cama; Baftan dos letras fin punto .

ca ma

Si a la ☰ fe pone punto arriba, dira.

que ma

Si a ambas abaxo ; dira.

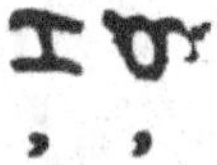

co mo

Las confonantes ultimas fe fuplen en todas las dicciones , i afsi para dezir, cantar ☰☰ . Barba ◌◌

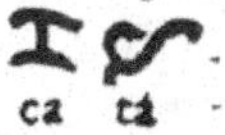

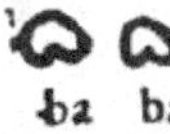

ca ta   ba ba

Pero conto do efo fin muchos rodeos fe entien , i dan a entender
mara-

FORMATION OF COMMON CHARACTERS

As observed by many authors the Philippine language has many affinities, knowing one makes learning easy,

The element that appears to be patent is the simplicity and the mechanism of the grammatical concept which are short, easy to understand and to explain, the phrases are formed by following the ordinary course of the idea which are clear to the end; these are perfectly pronounced and understood even in mispronounced words.

However, it should be known that precisely treating this idiom are various due to its glutinate character.

As the idea penetrates, the concept of the word finds the expression complete signified by a representative element of the idea in it and other representatives idea that are subject to modification.

The dipthongs _ay_, _ey_ _au_ are frequent but the Pampangos substitute the word for _aldao_ which they consider sweet, soft and clear.

The frequent use of the passive voice instead of the active is noted, and is determined in the frequent use of three conjugation in the passive voice _i_, _an_, _in_, that is arbitrary.

Equally common in the Philippine language is the absence of the Spanish z, ll, f, and the stronge guttural r of the strong consonants

As to pronouns a little difference exists between the use of the pronoun _tu_ among the Tagalogs and the Visayans. The pronoun tu in the Visayan idiom is always second person, equal of ranks or age of a person. Among the Tagalogs _tu_ is used in the second person among his equal or inferior ones, _cayo po_ is used in the second or third person to superiors and parents (equal to sir,) a sign of respect.

With regards to phonetics the simple elements are all equal as it occurs in the characteristic sounds represented by _ng_ to avoid cacaphony, example mabuting tao (good man) in Tagalog, although it would be correct to say _mabuti tao._[83]

---

[83] Barreiro – opinion cited page 36. In reality, W.E.R. Retanan said that ng is not a word but a

In the language of flexion whose roots are represented through phonetic variations, all the ideological relative values could not aid in the brevity, elegance neither in the variety of style and thus resulted in repetition and makes the figure of speech diffused and tiresome.[84]

In reality there is only one conjugation of the verb, but the Philippine language is impressive according to many authors. Mas said, " there are various due to some particular case as when verbs are united, or placed before or intermixed which fixed idea for modification and significance of a particular one."

These particular ones are nineteen, but actually are without senses, noted as mono syllables that cannot be put aside and are always in the formation of the words. Their numbers. vary from Malaysia, Caroline, the Pampangos, the Tagalogs and the rest of the Philippine idioms which are more advanced than the ones cited above. It is observed that, while the prefixes and suffixes are in the monosyllables, the disyllables and trisyllable are in major use., 2)

It is observed that in the language of the Philippine, the gender is common and there is only one delineation of the substantive noun and adjectives.

The tenses of the verb are hardly different in their endings. Thus in the tagalog language we have the following examples:

Ako'y bumibili	I buy
Ikaw bumibili	you buy
Siya bumibili	he buys
Tayo bumibili	we buy
Kayo bumibili	they buy
Silay bumibili	they buy

---

character of the alphabet and neither ng joined together but a diverse element and a consonant that has a sound. To designate this as a word a moderate dash should be placed on top. - W Retana-Apartado Bibliographo page 60

[84] However, Father Chirino said "the Tagalog language, no doubt is more courteous, artful, grave, and elegant because it shared the four qualities of the four major language world: Hebrew, Latin and the Greek and Spanish.

Like in other languages a single verb can be expressed in many ways. Examples:

(a) to see or to look .... alagby

(b) nothing .... aninao

(c) turning the head .... irap

(d) looking with malice .... irap

(f) to look angrily .... Rying

Mas said there are twenty of the above.

There are 42 ways to say "to put or to place."

75 ways to say "fasten."

Mas — opinion cited page 3-4

(c) Literature

Literature is the natural consequence of the written language of a nation. Recorded in annals and chronicles of the missionaries, the Philippines had a culture which was marked in their literary works or writings where moral truth and human passion were portrayed.

Thus the literature of our ancient forefathers consisted mostly of moral writings legends and myths. Those authors of antiquity recorded written traditions about wisdom beneficial to human life, treasures of prayers, songs about love and sorrows.

The Philippines was considered by the Spaniards as an indigenous people possessing epic poems in the style of the Illiad and the Grecian Ode, that sang the glories of its people and the memorable deeds of their heroes. Among the epic poems we have the Hud and Alim of the Ifugaos, the Biag ni Lam Ang of the Ilocanos, the Indaraptra and the Daragan of the Moros as collected by Gale, Krueber and Dixonate.

Poems of love, grief, adventures and celebration of bountiful harvests were sang to the accompaniment of musical instruments.

There were written works about mythology and the early Filipinos' belief in cosmology and the origin of races, fables about plants and animals, the legends of their tribes, spirits they worshipped etc. Interestingly their myths and legends bore traces of Hebrew and Hindu influences. For example, the history of the deluge of Northern Luzon and the legend of the Manubo Ango in Agusan contained some parallelism with biblical history of Lot and the Hindu myths of Ahalya in the Ramayan.

The ancient Visayans' mythology created a world they called *Bambu*.[85]

At the beginning of creation only the birds of prey, the sky and the sea existed. One day the birds, considered kings of the sky, got bored and persuaded the sea to make war with sky. The sea hurled huge amounts of bricks and earth which became nutrients of the

---

[85] Paterno, La antigua Civilization Tagala.

land. Out of the fertile land grew a tree which bore a seed fruit called Bambu. The Bambu seed contained the essence of things. When the birds cracked the Bambu seed a man called lalake and a woman called babae came out of it. These couple produced many children. When they got tired of their children, they started killing them. The children fled from their parents, running to the various parts of the earth. From these children came the existence of various races and their extensions.

The nobles hid in the interior of the woods where they became wasteful and fruitful. The Timawas hid among the rocks where they worked to get their food; those who had no place to go became the slaves. The blacks hid in the top of the mountains. The whites were the Spaniards who separated through the sea, and no one returned till the descendants came back.

Another literary tradition was about the Baliti a corpulent tree with a colossal elevation. According to accounts the *Baliti* was the favored home of the Nonos, the spirit of the dead, because of its magnificent crown. They also believed that it was there that the salvation of humanity could be found. Two youths fell in love, fled from the habits of evil men and lived in the trunk of the baliti tree for many years. There they grew all kinds of plants and raised many animals. Heavy with water the nodes broke and overflowed the spherical land. Aside from literature our ancient people had prophecies, refrains and superstitions.

With regards to the drama there existed a general opinion that it was taught by the Spaniards, However, E. delos Santos demonstrated that the Tagalog theatre predated the Spanish rule. Drama consisted of dances and poems set to music. Romantic love and conquest formed the principal plot of the plays. The Kumintang is an example of such a drama.

Fragments of these presentations are still preserved today, like the *ayok* or the *mabayoka* of the *Moros* of Mindanao. The embayok is a debate in poetry between a man and a woman. It's modern version in Tagalog is the balagtasan, in Ilocano it is the *bukanegan*, and in Pampango it is called *crissotan*.

(C) A Short Literary Resume

With aforementioned summation of the different authors, both

ancient and modern, our research made many author's book as ar
anti-thesis of our ancient history. Like epistles, we referred to them for
they are the authenticated records of our past history. We discern them
as facts of the unknown pages of our past history, dissipating the under-
current of falsities that had lain for many centuries.

In our research, we adjudged that many authors had the benefit
of using works of some authors for their history making. But it is sad
to say that the work they had written were not subject to scrutiny
and correct interpretation and thus became a precedent that was
not axiomatic; surely, we felt the frustration about important truths,
yet we found ourselves unable to prove unless we boast of
immutable evidence.

It is hardly necessary to say that the production or the making of
a book of merit and skill or excellence in every detail, calls for an
extraordinary research and organization. So subjectively we pen-
etrated the past; and posing as experts, shared great thoughts and
insightful facts from the beginning to the present, lacing the information from facts in every norm of the people being studied.

We have held steadfastly to the cardinal virtue of history
making: accuracy of truths and comprehensiveness. To attain this,
we consulted all sources that were relevant to our work.

From history and religious books, magazines, periodicals and
newspapers, an introspective survey in the norms of people of the
past and the present were studied.

"Truth is more wonderful than fiction and truth is the construction of the past". As we have said that science has opened the
realm of the past; like Diogenes lantern of his blinded lady, the
archaeological excavation done recently in our land lighted our
knowledge of the past which was recorded in In Nature's Bible buried under the ground; where intricate stories were like hypnotic tales
of legendary stories. It is a fact that things gone by impress itself
indelibly upon our minds and out of these truths, poets transformed
them into poems and sonnets on the miracles of the past.

Knowledge of the human race has been recorded and preserved

in said Nature's Bible and as men turn its pages; they will read the past colossal struggles out of which the present generation was born.[86]

What could be the motive of these men from the Asian mainland in coming to the Philippine archipelago, fifty thousand years before Christ? Could it be accidental, or charted by providence?

Though some twisted logic has turned truth against itself, we contend that it was a charted one and for a universal purpose.

The economic social progress and the spiritual receptivity of our ancient people were not vague facts.

(ii) Laws

Law is not abstract. It is not a force by itself. It is a creative form and can be presented in various significances. It is made for men and not men for the law. The jurists distinguised them in its general and formal aspects. In general sense, the law that comes from within and in the formal one comes from without. The general ones emanate from the moral laws within. Men know what is good and what is bad, and men are always inclined to do what is forbidden. Since freedom gives men the prerogatives to obey or to disobey, moral laws are then made with certain restrictions and impositions to bring about every ideal of goodness for the moral education of mankind.

These laws from without were promulgated by the Datus who, besides having political powers as well as judicial, also made laws. In many cases, it was believed that they were advised by the elders who were usually the chiefs or principals of the town.

These laws were made known by persons dedicated to this end. They were called Umlohocan, who proclaimed the laws to be

---

[86] Napoleon Hill, Law of Success. The pages of this Nature's Bible are made of the physical elements of which the earth and other planets consists of either with space. Turning the pages written on stones and covered near the surface of the earth on where we live, men has uncovered the bones, skeletons, foot prints and other unmistakable evidence of the history of mankind and animal on this planet; planted for the enlightment and guidance of Mother nature through unbelievable period of time. A plain and unmistakable evidence p. 17.

followed to the letter. This meant vigilance of the laws.

When the first Spaniard arrived in the Philippines, we had a government with laws and order. The foundation of a society will collapse unless it is securely set upon the fulfillment of good moral laws that give initiative for self-reliance and self respect. Laws and order enforced by justice strongly lays the foundation of civilization. Without the habit of order and the stern enforcement of the law at the expense of those who defiantly resist them, there can be no progress towards the growth, material or moral in civilization.[87]

In view of the Maragtas and Kalantiao Codes brought to the Philippines by the two Bornean Datus, it is inaccurate to claim they were edited by our forefathers. If ever they were adopted as our laws, it should be called Philippine Bornean Codes, like the Spanish Philippine Codes by the Spaniards.

The measure of these codes may be taken accurately by the extent they were adopted. Through the operation of the Graeco-Roman culture, as gleaned from ancient records of our forefathers, we are not in concurrence that these codes were adopted by our ancient people, for it has rather the characteristic of an anthology that has not shown a revealed religion. It lacked the progressive deepening respect for a human person, the inculcation of human feelings and the kindness that are seen in humanitarian laws. Records had shown that the hand of fate had long before reached the Philippines for our humane laws.

The arrival of the men from the Asian Mainland had foreshadowed the culture and traditions of our ancient people. The homogeneous narrations of ancient authors had not broken the context of incidents in their daily lives. It made possible for us to get the truths and ideas on broad lines of special viewpoint and characteristic of our forefather, these were not vague results. It had shown to be a filial and trusting journey. Traditions and the way of doing them both indicated that Someone Noble had been in the center of their lives as seen in the magnanimity of their work to serve others. The lofti-

---

[87] The Free Citizen, Herman Hedora form his collections and the ideas of Pres. Roosevelt, p. 140-141.

ness of their work was observed as they benevolently welcomed the Spanish explores upon their arrival in the archipelago. With love in their hearts, their generosity charmed the Spaniards.

We have observed, based on historical findings, that Infinite Wisdom and Infinite Love guided our ancient people on their onward course, Their malleable spirits and cultured thirst for knowledge and growth pre-disposed them to Christianization under Spanish rule.

This is the deepest mystery of our ancient history which has been blighted by misconceptions. However, it must be admitted that one's conviction on this theory, and the mental attitude in which one approaches it, make an enormous difference. To understand and grapple with this has been a major task in our conceptual range. It showed an element of faith, for the role they had shown a rare ability to embody the unattainable.

Paradoxical as it may sound, we believe that deep spirituality dwelt within them; a civilization had taken roots earlier and was already in full bloom when the Spaniards touched their shores.

Exposure to Hellenistic civilization[88] created a positive impact on the lives of our ancient people. Hellenistic culture exposed the Filipino to art, crude as they were, but representative of their era. It hastened the Filipinos' transition from barbarism to culture. It also instilled a deep sense of right and wrong, also known as morals, in them.

The wonderful precepts of this Hellenism were woven to the rich tapestry of our culture that had stood the test of time and made it strong and beautiful in the fires of life. It had a high degree of culture and a profile of attractiveness that significantly differed from the rest of their best Asian contemporaries.

Confirmed by the fascinating comment of Stanley Karnov which was thoroughly documented in his book, "In Our Image", where he said," Both the United States and Spain tried to shape the Phillippine

---

[88] Hellenism is characterized by the pursuit of art and special interest in philosophical reflection with morals and religious problem.

in their own image, but part from the American English and Catholicism, they never made their mark much below the surface." The popular summation was that "the Philippines lived three centuries in Catholic Convents and fifty years in Hollywood."[89]

Our unequivocal culture are living witnesses for they resonate with the total commitment of the present.

There are countless angles to explore but the foregoing facts herein mentioned are the gospel truths of our ancient history and therefore make it the Chronology of our ancient Philippines.

---

[89] Reprinted from the U.S. Based Catholic Reporter, 4/6/90.

Chapter III

LAWS AND GOVERNMENT

From the beginning of time people had some ideas how to deal with the external power affecting their lives. Although knowledge was scanty in the epoch, nevertheless, we can appreciate where the principle of these early people rested through the study of their beliefs and customs which have been preserved to the present time.[90]

Marriages among relatives of maternal parentage were forbidden by the primitive social groups and relations and unions were regulated outside their groups.

The patriarchal organization was produced by the domestication of animals and the pastoral life represented a superior one in the social development. Its form was more lasting and permanent in political formation. The pastoral and abundance of food ended their cannibalistic practice.

In the patriarchal system, the father was the head of the group and his power was almost despotic ; every one descending from the father, including the women, became members of the group. Members became united by the family ties, real or imaginary and authority within this group was personal. With the patriarchal system appeared slavery where the vanquished were pardoned and made to served their captors.

According to R. Getell, political unity was formed by uniting extensive units and others through consolidating by force.

---

[90] Historias de las ideas Politicas by R. Getell page 58.

The tribes were divided when they become extensive or were formed into confederation by the conquerors.[91]

Alliances were temporary and difficult to maintain due to the passage of time. They had no permanent union based on consent.

We are dealing in a science of pre-history particularly the civilization of the Philippines in pre-Spanish time so we mapped the right path in its history, government, religion, and education, all related with each other, and which gave rise to the unfolding of our civilization.

We observed in this work that annals and records have kept our institution keyed up to the Graeco-Roman institutions of the Middle Ages of Europe and gave us the fact that due to its geographical situation it had not escaped the great event of the global diaspora of the civilization started by Alexander the Great (336-323) B.C. Records then showed that civilization itself owed its existence to this significant event, which we think lighted the world and ended the dark ages of the world.

Undoubtedly, our government form has benefited from this event. We consider this event as the "the Hand of Faith".

---

[91] R. Getell-opinion cited page 80.

A INSTITUTION OF PUBLIC RIGHTS

(A) GOVERNMENT

In the exposition of our government, we followed a system that classified the institution in relation with people's public rights and private rights. From the documents of the Philippines we noted that since there was no data on established institution in any field, this classification is modern.

A complete vision of this political reign on the arrival of the Spaniards was described by J.P. Antonio and cited by Paterno:

"These people are not wanting in the management of their government; it was not simple at all for it was not monarchal for it lacked an absolute king; it could not be democratic for there were not many that governed the republic; it was aristocratic for here they had the *Maguinoo;* the government was divided".

Nevertheless, the concurrence of many authors was that it was anarchical where only the strong dominated.

Some towns had policemen without any political government, for an island or town knew no master, nor was under the care of a government. But those who conquered dominated. This resulted in the division, for the defense and fortification from invading guerrillas and ambush. The above opinion is only a part of F. Chirino's narration about the existence of a confederation. [92]

There were numerous narrations indicating that the level of Philippine politics was not inferior. It was comparable to medieval Europe and the politics the last days of the Arabs' reign in Spain. The government of Mindanao is an example. Although theoretically the supreme authority was in the sultan as the town chief, its government was sufficiently strong to be fully independent. These independent communities received the name *Balangay or Barangay,* independent in principle from each other, like the communities of ancient Greece. [93]

---

[93] The old confederation was known as the Mada-yas in Panay in pre-Spanish realized in XIII A. D. by the immigrants of Borneo.

[94] The name Balangay was converted by the Spaniards to Barangay.

The name *Barangay* was erroneously used to refer to a boat because the Malays were said to have arrived in the Philippine archipelago by boats with their chiefs. *Balangay*, according to the practice in Greece referred to groups of people or communities with a head or a chief. Father Collin described the government and the political customs of the islands as divided in *Barangays* in the rural areas and *Colaciones or Paroquia* in cities just like in Greece or Rome.

Because of its simple mechanism, it is now adopted by the Philippines as it opened the door to amicable settlement and solved many disputes before it reached many stages of litigations. The procedure was democratic as the chief was usually elected by the members of the group. He was called Barrio Captain and acted as a judge and moderator. When cases were not resolved, it was then referred to the proper authorities. This Balangay system was very practical and saved money and time. Only lack of harmony cooperation and unmitigated problems reached the court of judges. It is a lamentable fact that it took us Filipinos many centuries to recognize this laudable form of government.

Opinions varied among authors on the names given to authorities on different towns or islands.

One of the most common names was the *Datu*, that was distinct according to place. One was *Hayde or hari* that signified king or maguinoo second in authority. But in general term, the Datus were the political leader or chief.

Among the Moros, the term *Sultan, Datu* and Rahja were dominant.

Among the Ilocanos, according to Isabelo de los Reyes, "the corresponding name to designate superior authority was *Agturay* or *Aris*. The secondary chief was called *Amaen or Panglakayan*.[94]

Beside the political chiefs, the supreme legislator and judicial was the commander of the army. According to Morga his duties were to govern the subjects. They were venerated and respected

---

[94] Isabelo de los Reyes, **History of the Ilocos** p.102.

in the army during wars and navigations in the farms, fisheries, their workplace and assisted in the house with punctuality. They paid tribute from their crops called *"buis"*, some more and others less. In the same manner, the descendants and relatives of their chiefs were also considered nobles and were respected.

The superiority and power of these principals over the Barangay were too much that they maltreated the inferior ranks. The children and properties of the inferior ranking members of the group could be disposed of, blamed, killed or made into slaves for whatever reason and the superiors were not accountable to anyone. The Datu's ministry was generally obtained through inheritance. This happened due to the inheritance of slaves, properties, influence and wealth of the parents during their rule. They succeeded in preserving the power, but there was no principal custom that protected the weak and defenseless heirs.[95]

According to Morga, we had succession of inheritance." If the chief is the lord or master of the Barangay, the eldest son will be the first in succession and if he had no son, the eldest daughter will take place and if there was no one, the succession will be back to the nearest relative on the parent side of the principal or chief."

In the absence of a king, the regency will transfer to the wife. The woman can execute the authority and inherit it to be given to the one she marries. Some queens had more power than kings.

The position of a Datu is not only through inheritance but also for his personal power strength and intelligence.

It was not a close institution in the style of the European monarchy, but a flexible one shared by everybody.

With regards to the authority of the Sultan, de Francia y Ponce de Leon tells us that in the theory the Sultans were the dignitaries who gave them respect, settled disputes and served like aristocrat subjects. They knew their supreme authority that they ought to pay tributes.

---

[95] Succesos Cp. VIII, p. 104

(b) Nobility

Nobility constituted the second element of political power. It was composed of rich and influential people in the community.

People who had never been slaves received the name *Mahaldica* which was synonymous to the nobles. This name was among the tagalogs. Among the Visayans, it was called Datu or Maguinoo, the terms given produced confusion

Among the Mahadileas, besides the King, were the Maguinoos or the prince sometimes called Gat or Great Duque or first chief or master. Some of these had come to us like Gat-Meytan, the Master of Bulacan; Gat'-Salian the Master of Malolos; Gat~Paguil the Duke of Sampaloc, etc.

In the Tagalog aristocracy, the principles of equality and liberty were accessible to all levels of society. There was no caste system. The doors of the nobility were opened to all who gave great service and deserved merits. The best citizens were chosen to lead the community just as Rome chosed its senators from the elite. Talent and valor filled high positions. This Philippine nobility was similar to those of the Europeans in the Middle Ages.

Beside the text given by Paterno, Father Santa Ines expressed in a clear way how the nobility was acquired: few were acquired through blood; they were acquired through industry and fortitude.

Matrimonial union were celebrated among the same class in the community, although marriage with allied communities existed.

The nobility inherited important posts; ranks were inherited.

The concept of starting from the bottom of the rank and passing through the stages of chiefs or Maguinoo was unheard of.[96]

This chapter revitalized and emphasized the Graeco-Roman institutions, where authors continuously compared our ancient institutions with those of the institutions of Medieval Europe. The records and data interpreted these without any error. They were therefore, undisputed plain truths that were made inconspicuous

---

[96] Cronica de San Gregorio by Santa Ines, p. 56

and overlooked with indifference. But somewhere in the hearts and soul of our ancient people the respected culture of the West was planted.

It therefore behooves us to be thankful that the kindly hand of fate had reached us in the period of our ancient history; a history that has been shrouded by illusion, contentions, presumptions and misinterpretations.

Turn your thoughts to the hand of fate
Learn all things about it;
Be ready to proclaim them
and break the shrouds from within.
Look beyond the horizon
It has a language of its own;
Doth he came to lead the nation
Tis nature's plan for men's salvation.

THE FILIPINO RIGHTS

Right is a natural ordination of human conduct and is a social[97] manifestation as a result of a superior cultural stage. In the primitive stage, individuals resolved their disputes through force. In spite of certain manifestations in their self defense, individual relations in the Philippines were found to be regulated by the judiciary and were not confused with religion, which was usual in the origins of towns. Generally in the orient, a high grade of civilization was found. Nevertheless, religious influence was pronounced.

The primitive source of the Filipino rights were from customs and traditions. The grade of perfection acquired in the formal expression of laws makes us remember the great towns of antiquity, the rites of ancient Rome.

---

[97] Opinion cited by F. Collin.

Behind their lives larked earth
born activities,
A noble quality of people who
went beyond their years.
Their customs were without peers,
peaceful·and lovely,
A kind of Fairlyland with its
poetic beauty.
Seemed created by someone rather
than chance of history.
They knew their rights and limitations
In wonders of Nature they had
God's Laws in operation.

The last stages of pre-Spanish Philippines had no recorded details of the people's rights. Only the Bornean Codes of Kalantiao and Maragtas were found.

With regards to the Filipino rights, F. Collin said that "their laws and policy to be called barbaric were not very barbaric for it consisted of customs and traditions which were guarded with punctuality that could not be broken in any manner, as like respect for fathers and elders, so much that the names cannot be pronounced as in the customs of the Hebrews with their goddess."[98]

(1) CUSTOMS

Custom is a normal process created and imposed by social use. It is a more simple manifestations of rights and therefore from it sprung norms of conduct by a group of people.

In the Philippines, oral laws constituted the customs and traditions called *ugali* that were transmitted from generations to generations.

The major analogy was regulated by customs that in many cases were laws or a mere compilation of customs which were laws in itself presented in the form of precepts and imposition from without, which the Philippine tradition held firmly and with constancy continues to hold.

Although the narrations of the ancient authors were imperfect, nevertheless, they had shown that "Time the master worker" had a hand in the gradual education of the Philippines; a mysterious feat that made the archipelago "the oasis of Christianity" denied to the rest of the Asian nations.

CODE OF MARAGTAS[99]

The most ancient body of laws known in the Philppines was the Code of Maragtas named as such because it was found in Maragtas, in a pre-Spanish chronicle in Panay Islands. It was in Sanskrit and signified a "great town". According to investigators

---

[98] Ibid.

[99] Pormacion y Evolucion de las Razas Indonesia y Malasia, p. 374.

as well as learned Filipinos, unanimous opinions indicated that it was written in 1250 by Datu Sumakwel, the oldest and wisest Datu of Borneo who conquered Panay Islands. For this reason, it was sometimes called Code of Sumakwel. The following is the complete text:

I.   Deliberate refusal to work in the fields was a serious crime with a major penalty.

(a) Lazy persons were arrested and sold to the wealthy to serve as slaves to learn the value of work in the house and in the fields.

(b) When a lazy person had learned to love work he was returned to his family. His purchase price was returned and he ceased to being a slave and began life as a free man who like the fruit of his labor.

(c) But afterwards, if it was found that he was not completely reformed, he was rearrested by the authorities and sent to the mountains and was not allowed to associate with the rest of the community for being a bad example.

II. Stealing of any kind was punished severely by cutting the thief's fingers off.

III. Only those who can support a family could be married and have children.

(a) Poor families could not have more than two children because they could not support them and the community could not maintain them.

(b) The children who could not be maintained would be killed and thrown to the river to drown.

IV. If a man had a son with a woman and then abandoned her, the child should die because it would be hard for the woman to support her child.

(a)   The woman's family will disinherit her.

(b)   The authorities would capture the man and force him to marry the woman and if he refused, he would be executed with his son. Father and son will be buried in one tomb.

THE CODE OF KALANTIAO

The second oldest code known in the Philippines is the Code of Kalantiao edited in 1435 after the power was handed to Kalantiao Raja Desar. It consisted of eighteen precepts which were curiously compiled by the Recollect Father, Jose Maria Pavon.

The following are its precepts:

(1)   Do not kill, steal and offend the aged, for those who violate these will be exposed to the danger of death; they will be thrown to the river with stones or thrown into boiling water.[100]

(2)   Be sure that your debts are paid promptly. Those who failed will receive hundred whips by the chiefs for the first time and if the debts were considerable, they would be submerged three times in boiling water; for the second time, death penalty would be applied to him.

(3)   Nobody could marry a very young girl, or marry more than one if he could not afford or live in excessive luxury. Those who would not obey to this order would be ordered to swim for three hours; for the second offense, he would die with spikes of thorns.

(4)   Follow and obey so that peace in the cemetery and its sepulcher are not disturbed, and passing through them wherever they are in trees or in caves, respect should be demonstrated. All who disobey this will be exposed to ants until he dies; or of beatings or death to spines.

(5)   Contract about money exchanges should be complied according to the letter. Those who would not comply with the disposition would be lashed for an hour, for the second time he would be placed among the ants for a day.

(6)   Respect sacred places and other places known for their merits. For the first offense, he would pay a fine equivalent to one day's work in gold or molasses; for the second offense the punishment would be five years.

---

[100] Taken from the work of Almonte.

(7)   Death penalty was imposed on the following:

(a)Those who destroy venerated trees.

(b)Those who shot arrows at night and to the aged man and woman.

(c)Those who would kill sharks and crocodiles.

(d)Those who entered the house of chiefs without permission.

(8) Penalty for slavery was a daon, which signified time, for those who robbed the properties of the women of their chiefs; those who burned their neighbors' plants.

(9)   The following would be beaten for two days: those who sing on nocturnal nights; those who would kill birds called "Manuals"[101]; those who would destroy the documents of their chiefs; those who mislead with bad intentions; those who made jokes with death.

(10) It is the duty of the mother to teach sexual hygiene to her daughter to prepare her for marriage or motherhood.

(11) Husband should not be cruel or castigate his wife for committing adultery. Those who would disobey this mandate would be cut to pieces and thrown to the rivers.

(12) The following would be burned alive: those who through force and cunning evaded the punishment; those who robbed women, chiefs, and the landowners.

(13) The following would be put on ant mounds for a day: those who would kill cats during the full moon; those who would steal from chiefs or mayors no matter how insignificant the objects were.

(14) The following would be sentenced to perpetual slavery: those who would impede the marriage of their beautiful daughter to the son of their chiefs or masters and hide them with bad intentions.

The Visayan described their Manual with the bill of the parrot, a crown to pronounce the word. It lodged on trees believed to be the enchanted persons whose food consisted of chickens, mice and lizards.

(15) Concerning beliefs and superstitions: those who would eat sacred insects and plants would be lashed; those who would kill or harm the "Manual" or the white monkey would be whipped.

(16) Fingers would be cut: those who would destroy idols or put mud in their altars; those who would destroy sacrificial instruments used in their altars.

(17) The following would suffer the pains of slow death: those who would profane sacred places where they interned sacred things of their gods; those who defecated on sacred places would be burned to death.

(18) Those who would disobey the expressed precepts would be stoned to death and if they were old, they would be fed to the crocodiles in the rivers.

(C) ADMINISTRATION OF JUSTICE

The concept of the administration of justice as a phenomenon follows the doctrine in the division of power; the assimilation of the judicial power is not applicable, in the strict sense of our ancient civilization.

We used this term for it is commonly used or employed to designate the activity to judge and execute what is to be judged.

With this term, state and government also appeared. Since the existence of organized power, we could say in general terms that the state, government, etc. existed although it is not in the strict sense of what we have today.[102]

CIVIL DISPUTES AND CRIMES

In pre-Spanish Philippines, no clear difference existed between civil and criminal cases as the judiciary had an independent regulation for being contrary to the *penal indole* (judicial disposition). It is but natural, for this distinction is of the modern epoch.

We found no laws in the Philippines from which we can deduce

---

[102] We usually utilized them equally in our exposition of various terms.

or assume the existence of a legal distinction between the two cases of robbery and theft. These laws that governed them uniquely considered the mere act as a crime without distinguishing them if it was movable or immovable.

PROCEDURE

The parties that felt that they were aggrieved asserted their rights by petitioning the Judge for justice. In some cases, litigants appointed themselves as arbiters in a particular case or in a different Barangay or town.[103]

Before the arrival of the Spaniards, the primitive self-defense had completely disappeared. However, in certain institutions or persons they were preserved as we will see later.

To settle conflicts of interest between individuals in the same Barangay, Judges or Datus presided at hearings assisted by the elders.[104]

We could call this in modern terms as jurisdictional activity; this was not the only form used for the satisfaction of the parties. As we have said in the beginning, the arbitrary institution was known as an intermediate form, between those which we call today jurisdictional and judicial self-defense.[105]

CRIMES

In all organized communities, series of processes existed that provided deterrent to pernicious activities, protect property interests and helped avoid cases that produced crimes and levy punishments.

Anarchy laws of the ancient Filipinos were gathered from customs and laws.

---

[103] Historia de Ilocos, page 117 by Isabelo de los Reyes.
[104] Opinion cited by F. Collin, page 68.
"Jurisdiction" according to Professor Prieo Castro is the realization of the state for the realization of the judicial order by means of the application of the right that translate the tutelage and security of the particular rights.

However, we should be certain that the transgression considered damaging and punishable by the society is confined in the community that produced it. In the ancient Filipino rights, the crime operated in the confines of the community. On the contrary, rapes, abduction and piracy referred to other external community or enemies, pertained to acts of heroes and were dignified to be imitated and considered brave.

The study of these acts, considered as crimes by Filipino rights, is a sufficient matter for an independent work.

We will offer only a vision of allied acts since this subject belongs to specialists of judicial science.

The classification we made about these cases is not exhaustive nor a rigorously systematic analysis of judicial principle ... uniquely, we adopted on what it permits us to a general idea of the important crimes gathered from the ancient Filipino rights.

We discerned various ways to obtain a classification. In crimes we considered the degree of the danger in proportion done to the society (quantitative judgement or qualitative judgment) or the type of disturbance to the institution.

Regarding Filipino rights, we encountered elements that permitted us to classify crimes as a result of the pre-established standards. Thus we saw the existence of a clear distinction between a grave offense and a lesser one or fault which were easy to distinguish due to the punishment.

In a rigorously judicial conception, all crimes affect the community. All voluntary transgression of the judicial order is an attempt against the community. However, there existed acts that tend directly or indirectly to disturb the foundation where the community stands. It does not treat to attack or put in danger the common good in general, but only the representation of the community.

In a regime where the power or authority was concentrated in a single person or institution, like the Philippines, the attempt against any of them fell within this group.

Likewise, crimes that disturbed relations could also be called crimes against the administration of justice.

CRIMES AGAINST PROPERTY

In the history of civilization, as soon as tribes passed the roving or nomadic stage to sedentary, it took a special importance in the protection of properties, whether movable or immovable, where the economic life of the community rested. We do not mean to say that there was no protection of properties before, but in the later stage, there was a major political force.

It was considered a crime against property to those who deprived the disposition and its fruits.

We encountered many or numerous laws in the ancient Filipino rights that dealt on the protection of the rights on properties.[106]

One process that demonstrated the advance in the Filipino rights was the conciliation, a motive in the enunciation process as a result of wars among families or tribes; no sentence was intended until a cited conciliation was procured.[107] If the parties did not reach an accord, they made oaths to the Judge or Arbiters to follow their decision to continue their case. The Judge or the Arbiter determined the institution that straightly guarded the Roman right of the *"litis contestio"*.[108] This happened in civil and penal matters on the subject of indemnification or agreement.

Requisite completed, the summary verbally examined the proofs and the principle of indemnification and demand reigned.

If proofs did not resolve the cases because proofs were both in their favor, or justification was not satisfactory, the case went back to its first stage.[109]

If one of the parties succeeded with his proofs and helped the manifestation of justice, the case was decided in his favor.

But if the loser did not conform with what the judge has given, the Agturay or the Judge will impose. With this, we can confirm by

---

[106] We included possessions here.

[107] The amount stipulated for the parties as indemnification for the damage suffered from the crime.

[108] The amount stipulated by the parties for the payment of the damage done

[109] Historia de Ilocos by Isabelo de los Reyes, page 117

comparison that the function of Judges were similar to the major parts of modern rights; thus, not only judged but also executed the judgment.

Thus the loser had no more recourse but pay what the Judge demanded.

With this it could be observed that the most grave cases could be pardoned if the criminal paid the fine or the indemnifications.

According to Isabelo de los Reyes, what was interesting was that the victor had only the glory of winning, for almost all the amount went to the pocket of the Judge. But in criminal cases, only half of the charges went to the Judges. According to the cited author, the principle of the loser paying the cost of the suit applied which both parties paid for the processing costs.

The proof could be by witness, or trial by fire or water (trial by ordeal).

According to the observation of Isabelo de los Reyes, proof by witness was a dignified practice in the juridical progress of modern rights. It was the indemnification of witnesses for their molestation to suffer in having to declare question not of their own. Another political institution that is remembered in the juridical customs of the European in the Middle Ages was the trial by "ordeal". This was enough independent proof to decide the soundness of the witnesses, if they were sufficient or not in existence. Although we could employ it to the question of what we call today civil in the major application of what we actually know constitutes criminal matters.

The foundation of this institution was the belief that their god would not permit the innocent to be punished or the truth to be revealed for the punishment of the accused. This cited institution corresponded to the epoch when the considerable influence was supposed to be moderated by divine influence, that could give a possible injustice through the application of the strict rights. From this it was supposed that there will be an exit of the innocent, for it was believed to be the divine will of their goddess. From this, the cruelty of the proofs damaged only the guilty.

Father Collin described the following procedure to find truths about robbery:[110]

(1)   The ordeal of the river

(2)   The ordeal of the boiling water

(3)   The ordeal of the lighted candle

In the ordeal of the river, the suspected ones dove in the deepest part of the river, each with a spear in hand. The first one to come out of the water was considered guilty. Many remained under the water for fear of being pronounced guilty, so many drowned. This was founded in the belief that the guilty had a divine curse.

The ordeal of the boiling water: the suspect was obliged to hold a stone which was previously placed in the basin of boiling water; the one who declined or whose hands were burned was considered the culprit.

The ordeal of the lighted candle: it consisted of giving each one a lighted candle with equal length and equal wick; the one whose candle was first extinguished was considered the guilty one.

In penal matters a special procedure existed to terminate the process without dictating the sentence. When the case was about robbery, the procedure was suspended. The following procedure was done:

Each of the suspects was obligated to pile a mound of cloth or leaves on the object they wanted to discover and announced that they would return the object with a promise to be forgiven by the owner. In another contrary case the suspect was subjected to another test and if found guilty, he had to pay dearly for his crime. If the object appeared, the case was terminated and consequently the culprit was not punished and no inquiry was made if the lost object did not appear, the case was subjected to legal proofs.

When the criminal case was homicide, the relation of the killer and the deceased was determined to see if they belonged to the

---

[110] The version of Loarga

same or different community or to another, or whether the parties were friends or not. The juridical consequences of this supposition were distinct. Father Collin said that if the deceased and the aggressor were all principals, their families would go to the house of the killer and war was waged between the families until the elders entered in the case as mediators. The amount of the gold to be paid was declared according to the mediator's appraisal following the established customs of the locality. The amount was divided in this manner: one half went to the judge and principal and the other half was divided between the woman and the sons of the dead.[111]

However, with the disappearance of the principle of self-defense in the Filipino rights, the powerful made themselves the judges in homicide cases and the inferior ones were reduced to slavery without any due process[112] although this was a consequence of the aristocracy rather than of a legal derivative.

This was the only form for the settlement of conflict of interest between Datus and Barangay in the same place, except in Mindanao where the conflicts were settled by their Sultan, although this acknowledgement was only theoretical among the same datus in the same islands or territory, considering them the same power when the force did not show contradiction.

This is what we call juridical power today. As between parties, juridical capacity was required to act, that is the ability of the member in the community to act as a confederation and in cases where too many friends were involved and impartiality could not be achieved, strangers were permitted to act.

Due to the simplicity of the processal rights and lack of lawyers, clerks and constables, a petition was not necessary. The litigating person did not know the presentation of the juridical institution nor the judicial form of civil or criminal cases.

Neither persecution existed in criminal matters in the ministry of crimes. In cases where the datus acted in their initiative and

___

[111] Cited by F. Collin, page 69.
[112] Conquista de las Visayas by Isabelo de los Reyes, page 34.

committed crimes against themselves and their properties skepticism or contradiction confirmed the accusatory character of the Filipino rights.

Perhaps this accusatory character of the Filipino rights is the cause of the absence of infanticide as Isabelo de los Reyes said. The mother herself committed the crime and no other person could claim the new born infant.

If the aggressor belonged to another community, it was observed that the situation in the Philippines was similar to that of the German people during the Middle Ages when they did not have the superior laws of their conquerors.

(B) INSTITUTION OF PRIVATE RIGHTS

Under this we studied the institution in which the modern systematic institution was considered to effect the primordial right of persons including the personal situation of the individual and the patrimonial reign.

PERSONAL SITUATION

In pre-Spanish time the individual as such had no abundant right as we know then in modern times. On the contrary the right of the individual in many cases was modified and restricted in various influences.

For better comprehension we developed this situation into two aspects since they were fundamental in the Philippines.

THE GENERAL SITUATION IN THE COMMUNITY

The community had a powerful influence in the individual where important consequences were derived as lack of liberty to pass another community was prohibited. This prohibition was extended to all members in general, although in some category and in inferior cases there were some tolerance applied.

Trespassing another Barangay was ground for war, unless there was a pact to pay the agreed price to compensate for the harm it had done to the trespassed Barangay. In this case the children were divided by half with the other half awarded to all the members of the trespassed Barangay.[113]

In the ancient pre-Spanish Philippines, not all members of the community enjoyed equal rights because the Latin formula called "Estatus Liberatus" was applied.

According to the above it is fitting to distinguish three groups of individuals. Father Francisco de San Antonio in his description of the Philippine community gave us the following class of people.[114] In the Philippine community there were several classes of people, aside from the Datu: the illustrious who were called "Mahaldica", the free who had never been slaves among those who were called "Pecheros", and the legitimate slaves.

THE FREE MAN

The German professor, Blumentritt, *from the book* of Hermano Placencia about the ancient Filipino community, said that the Tagalogs divided the freeman into vassallos: cabalangay, emancipados, timawas, plebes, the illustrious Mahaldicas and Maguinoos. Among the Visayans, the plebes were the timawas and the nobles were the Caciquis and Datus.

Paterno impugned this classification in the following terms[115] "... I believed the classification is not certain for cabalangay signified the same balangay."

Cabalangay is equivalent to co-townmate, a name composed of the prefix "co" or "ca" and "balangay". For example, "sama" in the word "casama" originated from companion; "bayan" meant town and with the prefix "ca", it meant "cababayan" or townmate.

"Maguinoo" could not mean plebe or commoner because it meant noble, high, costly and highly esteemed.

---

[113]In this respect Paterno said, "Among the Tagalogs, no one can pass another Barangay without paying a certain amount that had been appraised by the whole community that had been trespassed. There were more difficulties encountered if the transgressor were married.

[114]Author cited Vol. 1, page 159.

[115] Author cited – La Civilization Tagala, page 271.

"Mahaldica" could not signify plebe because the interpretation of "Mahaldica" was absolute freedom.

Paterno explained the error of Professor Blumentritt in the following manner: Although in ancient times the word "balangay" referred not only to a free man but also to slaves in the same balangay, nevertheless in the later days when the inhabitants' population increased, the word applied exclusively to the free man and not to nobles or the illustrious, who became the middle class individuals in the actual society which evolved. The terminology dispute was resolved in favor of Paterno.

It gives us joy and honor to know that non-Filipinos took pains in studying our ancient people. This followed the gist of the famous Chinese scholar, Sun Yat-Sen when he said, "Know more of each other and we will love each other more."

These classes of free man were composed of the cited nobles and other individuals who were not subject to servitude or slavery. Among the Tagalogs and the Visayans they were called "Timagua" and among the Ilocanos "Timawa".

Those who did not pay tribute nor render work to the Datus were privileged. They owned properties such as lands, houses and furnitures and they had the liberty to select their work or occupation. Their obligations to the Datus were absolute obedience, fidelity, submission, going with him to war, as well as accompanying him in hunting and fishing trips. Considered as companions, they received shares of the spoils.

NOT FREE

In order to appreciate the "not free" in the Philippines, we ought to make a fundamental distinction between the serfs and the slaves.

Both groups constituted an inferior sector in Filipino society. The Tagalogs called the slaves "aliping sangigilir"[116] and the serfs "aliping namamahay".[117]

---

[116] According to D' Almonte in Visayan, "ayuei" is a half slave -- a son of free men and a slave. Tomarampok. Cited by I. de los Reyes. The slaves were dominant in the Ilocos "Tagabu", "Adipen", "Katalonan".

[117] In the Visayan Tomataban.

Some authors confused Tagalog servitude with slavery, a case of serious error as observed by Paterno.[118]

Father Juan de Placencia in his work "Relacion de las Antiguas Costumbres de los Indios", written in 1589, was the first to make the distinction of the slaves down the stairs "aliping san guigigilir" and slaves who worked in the master's house as "aliping namamahay". Dr. Antonio Morga, who did not speak the language nor had gone near the Philippines to see the practice and customs of the Indios or the Tagalogs, followed this work, whose famous production the "Sucesos de las Islas Filipinas", was blindly copied by the Antonio de la Llave 1660, and by Father Collin in 1660 although he introduced some variations. Later this was absolutely believed by Father Juan Francisco de San Antonio in his work, "Las Islas Filipinas", as he declared in paragraphs 432 and 436 the first part of Book I, a work considered a gospel and copied by Mas and other European authors who treated it obliquely and thus resulted in grave opinions from authors whose pen were soaked in bad ink.

THE SERFS

The serfs were called the Aliping Namamahay or semi-slaves.

They were half slaves and half free. They had individual properties like houses, fields and servants but did not enjoy complete use of the products of their properties. Some parts of their products in spices or in gold were attributes given to their masters who could accept tributes only but could not sell or confiscate the serf's property.

Morga said that the others who lived in homes outside their masters' had to work out in the fields of their master as well as in the house without pay. Their children and descendants were slaves of this master.

The magnates and the principals who were the cause of the loss of their properties were given the above service. Others gave their

---

properties spontaneously to the opulent for their protection from the ignominy of the aliping namamahay.

Many freemen renounced their liberty and also put themselves under the protection of the Maguinoos (powerful) to avoid the pitiful loss of their rights as in the cases in Europe during the Middle Ages, where country people were oppressed by the nobles. They also gave their properties to powerful men of the church during Feudalism.

In the class of Alipin Namamahay, we could count on the *catipados* and the *cabalangay*.

Cabalangay were townmates or individuals who belonged to the same Balangay. Their servitude was born out of the contract they made with the Maguinoos, the principal head of the Balangay, and they had the obligation to serve when called to work in the fields or at parties. They enjoyed the drink of Tuba or quilang which was their wine. Thus, they gave the Cabesa the agreement in the pact.

In time of war, the Cabalangays were subject to the orders of the Maguinoos or principal who could call him to fight if he so chose. In this case the Maguinoo supplied the arms and the alcohol from the coconuts.

The lovers were called Catipados. The service arose from the desire to gain merits in the eyes of his sweetheart, and having no dowry to pay, the amount stipulated became servants of the future in-laws.

THE SLAVES

Among the Tagalogs the slaves received the names of Aliping Sangigilir which in the Tagalog language signified servants under the stairs (pronounces Gulir) that was inside the house or at its entrance.

Father Delgado continued[119]... among them were various kinds

---

[119] Delgado - Historia de Filipinas p. 350.

of slavery, because some of them were entirely slaves, some were half slaves, and fourth slaves. Father Collin referred to this, because if the mother and the father were free and had a son, the son would be half free and half slave. If they had more than one son, they were divided. The first would follow the father whether as free or slave. The same rule applied to the mother, The last two would be half free and half slave..

The descendant became only one fourth slave because the mother and father were only half free.

In some cases where two parties wanted to marry but the groom had no money to pay the dowry or to pay the woman, he was made a slave. Under this scenario the first, third and fifth sons belonged to the father for he was a slave of the mother. Upon the death of the father, the ownership of the brothers were partitioned. The second and the fourth belonged to the mother according to practice. She was like the master and principal of the father and brother, for he was slave of the mother.

In the works of Father Collin, the slaves constituted wealth that was much coveted. Like commercial projects, the more skillful slaves commanded higher and fixed price. Ordinarily, it was tales of gold ($1.25) in the Philippines, or 6.25 pessetas in Spain, or a weight of 30 grams. Those acquired in wars were sold but those born in their homes were not.

The fall to slavery was described by Father Collin:

The common organ of the fall to slavery was usury and speculation practiced by the father to son, son to father, relatives to relatives. No one helped each other although they saw the necessity. Without contracts, the borrower paid back in double amount when he failed to pay on time.. thus the debtor became a slave until he paid back his debt, which became impossible as the interest had multiplied according to the agreement.

Other slaveries resulted from tyranny and cruelty, made in vengeance by their enemies. In their encounter during guerrilla wars, the prisoners became slaves although they were from the same town, and same lineage. Slavery was punishment by the chiefs for minor offenses, such as failure to guard for what was ordered, making noise in the mortuary of the chiefs. The powerful took away the liberties of the miserable people and tyrannically made them slaves together with their sons and wives. Wars, debts, and punishments brought slavery to the lives of many people.

There were magnates who had as much as 300 slaves and because it was a specie of wealth more esteemed than gold, they wasted no time augmenting their slave-hold by waging wars with their neighbors, terrorizing even their own "pecheros" and Timawas on frivolous pretexts, as passing where the wife was bathing.

Interestingly different from other cultures', Philippine slaves had rights. They could have properties through their labors and from donations. When the work assigned to them were finished, they were paid for their extra work. They received gifts like jewels for their service and fidelity.

Work inside the house was not excessive. It was just what was necessary for their daily consumption and survival.

Slavery is a sad development in the life of the individual for it attacked the dignity of man. The greatest of Man's grief was the loss of his dignity as an image of God; greed and selfishness were the enemies of mankind especially when carried to extremes.

It is noteworthy that ancient authors had made chapters for admonitions, alternating with chapters of narrations about the relentless truths of our ancient people's adherence to morality before the arrival of the first Spaniards in our lands.

The distinctive features of the Philippine slavery was the guaranty of personal independence to own properties. It guaranteed individual freedom to work and earn after he completed with work assigned to him by his master and thus guaranteed or secured each slave's right to live and regulate his private life and affairs as he chooses. From the big heart of his master, he received a day off for every three days of work.[120]

---

[120] Opinion cited by Mas

According to Isabelo de los Reyes in the Philippines, slavery was not practiced so rigorously as in other European or Oriental nations. As assured by Father Rada, he heard slaves answered their masters in the negative, "I don't like", in response to his master's command.[121] What better sign of democracy could a country show, than the scene of a slave sitting as an equal at his master's table. Probably the best test of love of liberty in a country is proven by the way it treated its minorities, as Hermann. Hagendorn said in his book, The Free Citizen.

The practice of slavery had been interpreted as a manifestation of our forefathers' primitive stage. The Romans practiced slavery even before the coming of Christianity.

On the subject of slavery, we have what St. Paul said on the influence of Christianity in the institution of the day.[122] Christianity did not take up an external position of hostility to the institution of slavery on which the GRAECO-ROMAN world was based. It did not proclaim an economic and social revolution, but destroyed from within the mistaken assumption of the institution, and replaced them by principles which, once they were understood, could cause the collapse of the institution and in the meantime transform relations between freemen and slaves in the bosom of Christianity.

The existence of slavery in the Philippines indicated the disappearance of cannibalism and anthropology, and therefore was an exponent of the advance progress of the Filipinos in the high road of civilization.

Accordingly we have three distinct groups of individuals: the free, the serfs and the slaves.

F. Juan de San Francisco gave us in his description the classification of the Philippine communities. (1) The ranks of the people in those antiquity as given by Hermano Placencia, aside from the datus, were some noble man and woman who were called Mahaldica by the Tagalogs.... the free who had never been

---

[121] History of the Ilocos- Isabelo de los Reyes.

[122] Author cited T.I., page 159. The Early Church in the Acts of the Apostles - Msgr. Enrico Galbiate p. 223.

slaves... the pechero or commoner, and others who were legitimate slaves.

(B) PATRIMONIAL REIGN

This topic corresponds to the development of a situation that constitutes the economic foundation of the community. With it we include the study of property and inheritance.

We will prove in Chapter V that the Philippines was in a stage of an agricultural civilization, being in the same base of property institution on the arrival of the Spaniards in the Philippines.

Property, a very important element in life, was regulated by laws and customs.[123]

Wealth, where the right of property falls, comes in various forms – from lumber, forest products, pasture lands, fishponds and as well as slaves, fall under properties.

The distinction between the individual property and common or community properties were known among the ancient Filipinos. The community possessed great extensions, in comparison to the individuals, where all members could benefit from it by following the norms of the customs that left a wide margin for initiative particularly given the wealth and abundance of the major common wealth of the archipelago.

In this particular case, Santa Ines said "every one knew his particular property and no one could plant or reap except the one who planted and the one who inherited the land even though it was outside their barangay".

Among the Tingians, the unirrigated lands in the mountains which were reputed to belong to a barangay were common property to all. The first who planted would be the one to reap and profit in that year and no one could disturb him; planting in a barangay of another man never happened.[124]

[123] Ibid. Agriculture.

* Ibid. – the following epigraph.

* Author cited in the La Antigua Civilization Tagala, p. 71.

* The Early Church in the Acts of the Apostles and in their writings by Msgr. Enrico Galbiate, page 223.

[124] Cronica by Santa Ines, page 57.

The common wealth were usually pasture lands, agricultural lands, forests and fisheries. Other particular properties existed. The private properties constituted of houses, slaves, furnitures, arms jewelries and lands.

INHERITANCE

Philippine customs and laws on inheritance were summarized as follows:

All legitimate sons inherit the properties of their parents; if there were no legitimate sons, the properties went to the nearest relatives, collaterally from the trunk of the family of origin.[125]

Isabelo de los Reyes wrote..." if a man legally married twice and had children from both the marriages, the property acquired during the respective marriages would go to the respective children born of each union".[126]

In the chronicle of San Francisco de San Antonio, the illegitimate child of a free woman inherited one third of his natural father's property.

The illegitimate child of a slave could inherit only furniture.

Morga said that illegitimate sons were only assigned some, but did not say whether the son of a free woman could inherit a third.

The son of an adulteress had the right to inherit like the legitimate sons, provided he had paid the indemnification of the conjugal injury; however, he had no right to inherit from his mother inspite of the fact that he lived with her.

SITUATION IN THE FAMILY

When the Spaniards arrived in the Philippine archipelago in the year 1521 A.D., they found the Filipino family patriarchal and completely developed within the historical period of the Patriarchal social evolution. The father being the spoke of the family, rendering

---

[125]Isabelo de los Reyes - Historia de Ilocos, page 177

[126] Sucesos - By Morga, page 303.

all time consideration to his wife, counsel or mistress, house governess, the children's mother who was responsible for bringing continuous joy to ease the burden of the terrestial journey.

The time of succession had brought about the embryonic stage of humanity which was dominated by the Tagalogs. It was the most patriarchal social life, the key to the historical evolution of the tribes, towns, cities and nations.[127]

As a consequence of these social evolution over a long series of years, communities, matriarchal and patriarchal, had been established so it was precisely important to record this in the remote past. On those times the son was not considered of equal status with his father. But after some time the son was generally allied to the tribe; the second time to the father and not to the mother and ultimately to the father and mother. Other marks of the remote past should not be confused with general and extraordinary situations because other residues of the past remain unknown like fragments of stones that followed the current of the rivers and remain buried in its beds which when collected would help geographers and historians reconstruct the passages of the primitive life of humans- like the discovery of bones of animals that paved the way for the study of plant life in the land.

There was nothing strange found in the human endeavor of our ancient people, although not a standard for the whole world. The different phases of their social revolution was not only at par but had excelled some of their contemporaries of those times. For this ancient authors had rewarded them through the continuous admonitions on what they found.

It is precisely important to present here that the Filipinos were firm sentiments of the Martriarchal system.

The Roman family was not considered as a family by the Filipinos (called Tagalogs by the Spaniards) in its sense because it was founded on power; while in Luzon, the family was founded on matrimony and parentage.

---

[127] La Familia Tagala - Historia Universal by Paterno, page 81.

The Filipino family was always attached to their ancient customs and were composed of individuals united by blood. Among the old Roman family, the vanguished made up the empire's family unit. For the Tagalog family, the wife, husband, sons, slaves and other were considered as a family unit.

In Luzon, a woman who entered the circle by the virtue of matrimony or in extremes, or by adoption was recognized as a regular member of the family, even though the family bond was not by blood.

Among the ancient Filipinos, their family link was completely defined. The children recognized their duties to their parents while the parents had almost perpetual care of their children from their day of birth. The parents continuously invoked the blessing of their god and their anitos for protection until the children were capable to live by themselves. The father governed the family unit as if it was a monarchy.

According to F. Chirino, the husband was the chief of all as seen in the Philippine customs, he was absolutely respected by the children. This old ancient tradition has been preserved to date. The obligation of obedience to parents continued even the children were already married.

ADOPTION

The Philippines had the custom of adopting legitimate sons of others although the biological father still lived. The adopted son had to give his legal father the amount stipulated in the contract (gold). Upon the death of the political father, he had the right to inherit and could collect double his inheritance if he wins the good grace of companionship. He could also inherit jewelries. If the adopted son desires to rescind his adoption, he had to return the gold and live without a father. In case the adopted son died before the adaptor, he became the absolute owner of the price of the adoption, inspite of the fact that the adopted father had children of his own. [128]

---

[128] Mas, Informe Sobre Filipinas.

According to Father Collin, there was also the practice of adoption of daughters through purchase. The biological father gave the adoptor a certain amount for having adopted his daughter. With tenderness and power of the home, she remained adopted and would inherit double the amount of the adoption price, that was if she was sold for ten, she would inherit twenty.[129]

MATRIMONY AND DIVORCE

The base of the Philippine family is rooted in matrimony. Among the ancient Filipinos, monogamy and polygamy were found, but no polyandry was encountered. The Negritos were found to be generally monogamous while the Moros and the Calingas were polygamous.

Matrimony in the Philippines constituted a tight bond among the conjugal spouses although there were possibly divorces. To them, marriages were indissoluble until the death of one partner, a foreshadowed command of our Lord.

The conjugal society of the Philippines was established over a social organization not of philosophical nor ephemeral (beginning one day and ending the same day) but of solid morals from father to son.

The most common and general practice of marriages was described by Father Chirino. The Visayans always married from within their lineage or one very close to their kindred. The Tagalogs married outside their lineage provided he or she was not inferior. They did not have any impediments and it was common to see uncle married to niece, first cousins to one another. There was no marriage between brother to sister, grandfather to grandchild nor father to daughter.[130]

According to Morga, "they married their own class — slaves to slaves, principals with principals, though sometimes they married and mixed with others".[131]

[129] F. Collin, Labor Evangelica.
[130] Chirino, Relacion, p. 70.
[131] Ibid.

Dr. Jose Rizal, our most learned Filipino, in his note about the work of Morga, interpreted the text by the following terms: "this proved that the relations among these classes were not seemingly far from the occidental nobility, but more cordial than the patricians of the Roman people .... among them was the prohibition among the principals to establish ties by means of marriage".

If the Filipino principal and the Timaguas were tyrants to their inferiors as had been painted, there could not be such unions; hatred and desertion would separate the classes".

They married a woman who was called <u>asawa</u> and she became the real owner and governese of the house. If in the past the man had a son with another woman, the son was considered the legitimate heir of the father. [132]

The husband gave the dowry to the father; the woman brought nothing to the marriage; however, she would receive an inheritance later.

This dowry, Rizal told us, represented the indemnification to the father for his forbearance of the education and care of his daughter. The Filipino wife had never been a burden to anybody, neither to her parents nor to her husband. In the contrary, she represented a value the possessor would have difficulty reconstructing upon the loss.[133]

With this we are certain that in our ancient time, the father had much concern for the pain of the loss of his daughter.[134]

In cases of divorce, Morga said, that ... the spouses separated and dissolved the marriage for light reasons —on the interviews, the opinions and soundness of judgement, the debts of both parties and the elders who intervened..." Dr. Jose Rizal wrote, "that those were more advance than the French and the English in their laws of divorce". Without touching the insolubility of marriage, we believed the judges made their summation of the debts of both parties;

---

[132] Morga, Successos, p. 301.
[133] Dr. Jose Rizal
[134] Ibid.

and in spite of returning the dowry, made the divorce convenient and light.[135]

The debts of both parties and the decision of the elders regarding the question on family matters were more sacred than the doctors and judges no matter how wise they were on the convenience and inconvenience of the unions.

Other historians among them, Father Aduarte noted, that when families had children, they never separated for the love of their children.

Paterno said that both the wife and the husband had the liberty to go to the Sonat or priest who married them, to ask for divorce. The priest tried to reconcile them as their ama sa ligao or sponsor. In the company of the parents and the elders who were appointed by both families, they decided to dissolve the marriage contract.[136]

In cases of the dissolution of the marriage Morga said, "the dowry was returned to the husband. But if he was the reason for the break-up of the marriage, the dowry was not returned but remained with the father of the woman.

The properties they gained were divided in halves and each one disposed of them. If they had animals that could not be divided, it was given to the consort.

---

[135] Morga, Ibid.
[136] La Antigua Civilization Tagala, page 308.

Chapter IV

RELIGION

The Philippines has known godliness since time immemorial. Although our histories were full of depreciations by other nations, the enigma of the Philippines as a towering figure of Christianity in the Orient was not affected.

At the time of the arrival of the Spaniards, they were not pagans. The term Christian is vague. They were not Christians for they were not born in a nominally Christian country. They were not baptized in a Christian church. They knew next to nothing of the Apostle's Creed, but they had a dignity independent of class education and rank. So deep were their religious belief that they were taught to worship another god.

They never dwelt in atheism; they never worshipped trees, calves nor the moon as the pagans did.

The careworn heart turns to religion for hope and encouragement proving religion was the backbone and outstanding power of the world and brought change to the human conduct in moral, social and business life. It is an apprehension or conviction of the existence of a Supreme Being or a more widely supernatural power or influence controlling one's humanity.[137]

In the history of religion, we have what Jesus Enciso said, " the history of religion is a conjunctive of beliefs and practices that has a fundamental of the speculative order in regards to the divinity of a person. The first constitutes liturgy and the second the fullness of morality.[138]

The practice gave the relation between God, himself and his neighbor. To avoid errors in this concept of paganism, Jesus Enciso's authoritative statement stated "when the Romans spread

---

[137] Int. Dictionary in Reference to History.
[138] Historia Comparadas de la Religion, page 67 by Jesus Enciso.

Christianity, they selected the best nucleus of civilization because it has the influence to society". So in this manner there was a time when false religion became the patrimony of the villages called in Latin "Pagus"; hence the word paganism.

Paganism therefore referred to all religion which adored a false god. Paganism did not refer to Judaism nor Mohammedanism as these religions believed in their "true" God. Treading on this vein of reasoning, our ancestral religion was not pagan because it adored what it believed to be a real God, they called Bathala or Maycapal.

"This theoretical principle and practices had come to a person in the practices of his natural faculties or by divine revelation. The first case was natural religion and the second was revealed or positive religion".

With this, no historical nation existed that professed a religion purely natural. All religions constituted some elements of real or false beliefs which they believed were revealed and received from Divinity that in the past had been revealed by their forefathers.

These revealed beliefs usually refer... in the doctrinal order in the intimate nature of divinity, geonology and its association with man in the moral order, added precepts to the natural rights, like the prohibition to take determined objects or to eat determined foods in the liturgical order and other minute accounts of the rites.

With respect to the ancient religion of the Philippines, we have what Father Delgado transcribed... "when the Spaniards arrived in the Philippines, they found no temples where they made their sacrifice and adoring false gods like other religion of heatheism, gentilism nor found a written work of religious doctrine nor a history of our past.

At this point, what they found was a tradition which was constant from father to son and vain works for gods; some of these have been published as "Folklore Filipinos".

In this chapter, annals proved that no religion existed in our lands except a religious foundation.

While researchers still fail to find the secret of our past, the Christian spirit was found among our ancient people. So, we are convinced that our quest will not fail if we resort to a religious outlook. Incredible as it will seem to irreligious men, this wonderful spirit which was significant in their ways of life, traditions and outward expression cannot be overlooked for we believed that God was with them in human form.

Our people were ordinary people. By nature, they spent their lives in simple ways, but they lived them in a special and extraordinary way that astonished authors who believed they were a mystical people.

By their deeds they were known
Solid and strong like diamonds,
A legend for centuries unknown,
Filled with love and joy.

Thus, we believed that the hospitality and godliness of our ancient people were the outward flow of the indwelling of God with our ancient forefathers long before the arrival of the Spaniards in our lands.

In Paterno's opinion, the Philippines got its Christian principle from the men who were in contact with St. Thomas in his missionary work in the East. But we believed that this Christian principle was ahead of the Christianization. Our thesis had an important significance on the introduction of morality and philosophy of life long before the arrival of the Spaniards and the spread of Christianity.

It was in morals that had a major measure for without it the rapid Christianization of the Philippines cannot be explained, considering it almost took a millennium before Christianity grew its roots in Europe.

If Hellenism had prepared the hearts of the Jews to welcome the teaching of Christ as propagated by the Apostles, in like manner we say that the men from the East prepared the hearts of our ancient people to welcome the teaching about Christ by the Spanish missionaries.[139]

The most priceless finding that could solve the mystery of the source of this religious foundation was the archaeological discovery of the arrival of sapient men from the Asian in the Philippines 50,000 B.C.[140]

This event, we believed, opened the secret of our ancient history. We too believed that these men were God's agents for our superior destiny to start His Providential Plan of Salvation.[141]

They came to teach, to convince and to mold,
In all areas we were told
Sent by someone of Old
Who worked together for good,
not faith alone was sown,
But men of grace accidentally found.

Throughout the thousand years of the relatively unknown existence of our ancient people they consistently remained in their pre-colonial bases when the Spaniards arrived in the Philippines. Our standpoint was always to scrutinize to the core for a well balanced account to support all aforementioned contentions. Our pre Spanish histories were made only through observations and recollections and unfortunately by foreigners. We made a trans-continental survey of our people with the rest of the world to avoid the conviction that this work repeated what many authors had done by copying that repeats itself. We did repeat many but we gave the adequate facts which were unprecedented in the history of our ancient people.

Our conclusions are entirely warranted despite our restrictions in many factors.

The character of our ancient people, their contemporaries and

[139] The early Church in the Acts of the Apostles by Msgr. Enrico Galbiate.
[140] Ibid.
[141] Ibid. The Acts of the Apostles in their Writings- by Msgr. Enrico Galbiate.

the recent excavations are the masterly interpreters of our ancient history. Throughout the ages our forefathers professed what we are the timeless secret that God was with them.

We have the following descriptions of the sacred names of our God as translated into practice by negative authors.

A. THE NAMES OF GOD

Paterno wrote that the most sacred name in the Tagalog civilization was the name of their God.[142] They called Him "Bathala". Unlike the Christians they did not pronounce it except in great respect and adoration in the most solemn moments.

Perhaps here came the error that the Philippines had no god and admitting it there was not only one but many whom they invoked as saints or anitos.

The Tagalogs followed the customs of venerating the Jehova and the Bramans and before one could pronounce the word, he had to prostrate himself upon the ground.

The mysterious name was written in the characters that corresponded to the Latin letters B.H.L. which was similar to J.H.V. in Hebrew Hehova.

B.T.H.L. read in reverse is LaHaBa.

The term Lahat means all; Babaye was the sign of generator-creator of all.

Father Juan de San Antonio in his famous description of the Philippine archipelago said that the Tagalogs adored many gods "but among all they respected and adored the principal the greatest of all whom the Visayan called Lauon that meant ancient (1) ang the Tagalogs called Bathala Maycapal that signify Creator Maker of all that existed".

---

[142] It is Bathala for the Tagalogs; Lauon for the Visayans, Akasi for the Zambals; Gugusang for the Bicols; Kabunian for Ilocanos and Igorrots.

It was observed that the name God was written in three consonants B.H.L. Bathala which was equal the Hebrew J.H.V. (Jeova).

It was also observed that the accent to form the expression of the word was in the second letter and this letter was the first and common. The H was pronounced with a full breath, a letter in a way to express the invincible the simple and the spiritual.

It was Bathala for the Tagalogs, Lauon for the Visayans, or Alba, Akasi for the Zambals, Gugurany for the Bicols, Kabunian for the Ilocanos and Igorrots.

In the Tagalogs' writing the letter "H" was written in imitation of the zig-zag lines unfastening the heaven that illuminate the dark earth, thus forming the graphic and spiritual exrpessions of light, that God created and conserved all things.

The ancient Tagalogs wrote Babae (woman) as an abbreviation, a symbol of generation; in like manner, Lalake (male) was written in T, an abbreviation.[143]

B. DOCTRINE OF GOD

The Philippine philosophical religious conception about God was based on the idea that God was the Creator.

Bathala was the unique substance of all actions and passions, everlastingly of genus one, genus two and genus three of all the universe.

With all these, things existed in the simplicity and multiplicity of all things. Nothing existed outside her, like the rain was the animation of the sea, that rose and returned to the sea. All divine emanations were born and returned to the sea where they were lost like the drops of rain in the immensity of the ocean.

These revelations of ancient authors of our ancient religion should make the supreme end of our quest, for comments of many authors of our religion showed that God lived in them. Inasmuch

---

''La Civilization Tagala, page 39.

as no missionary had done the missionary work, could there be still qualms from skeptics that the Diaspora of the Greek culture had reached the Philippines before the arrival of the Spanish. It had worked miracles throughout the ages and not surprisingly it had left a pertinent relevance up to our days. With the exhumed truth of archaeological excavations, perhaps the concept of a mystical people was made plaussible.

To avoid conflicts of information, we present here some more authors who painstakingly observed the notions of our forefathers' religion and the philosophy of life after death, one of which was a precept in the Greek culture that was started by Alexander the Great 336-323 B.C.

According to Santa Ines, "They had a place they called Meca as a place of paradise or town to rest for the just, the brave, those who did not harm anybody and other moral virtuous. They also believed that they had a place where bad people were banished to which they called Casamaan, a place of pain and affliction, where the devils habitate.[144]

He continued to say "that at the beginning of the world, was seen the vanity of the world, mixed with fables and lies.... and higher than the beautiful sun was the Languit (glory) where the Lauon (the most ancient); the just rose by the splendor of the sun (Balangao). There the soul of the just and the saints united; and there they were lost in the immensity of Bathala.

Rooted in the history of religion, men believed that there was a Supreme Being, creator of all things and men had been communicating with Him since the dawn of history for they were not natural atheists. Men were aware of Him and in fact wise men in all ages talked to Him in their minds."

As a Greek poet has said: "to an Unknown God"

"To Him we live and move and have our being, for we are indeed His Offspring."[145]

---

[144]Cronica by Santa Ines, page 50
[145]Aratos (Phenomena) – A Greek Poet.

"That He lifts men to unbelievable heights, the sun that radiates goodness, form beauty, the birds that sing and excite inspiration and produce admiration. For the evil men who causes the existence of hearts like stones and beasts with the intelligence of man. He is the tempest and the fire that devours and is the catalyst of death. God is the principal of all precepts and absorbed in its bosom all spirits but repeals away all bad spirits."[146]

C. MAN

"Also rooted in the history of our religious beliefs was man is a creature superior to all creations. He is in the world as an image of God and therefore has the power clothed by God to rule the world. The likeness in which He made man was not stated, but it is legitimate to think that it was with intelligence and will".[147]

On the other hand this passage cannot satisfy our scientific curiosity for our purpose is to find the progressive formation of the structure in the religious practice and beliefs of our people as described by the many authors like Paterno.

Based on the narratives of Paterno, we deduced our ancestors' religious beliefs and psychology about God and man were peculiarly akin to our present beliefs about God and man. It is of worthy commentary analysis and even emulation for neither any natural nor human reason can support these philosophical theories, unless someone unlocked their spirits with someone's cooperation.

Call it religion, psychology or chemistry. Their concepts of religion and philosophy of men were the following:

"In the first place it considered that man lives and thinks. In relation with the world there was nothing perfect in the land where he stands; that man is an atom in space; for an instant of time his body is turned to grains of dust; his life is a dream and his spirit vanishes with the splendor of the sun". (Arao)[148]

<hr>

[146] La Antigua Civilization Tagala by Paterno page 39
[147] History of Salvation – The Old Testament by E. Galbiate p. 36.
[148] La Antigua Civilization Tagala by Paterno page. 148.

About the Filipino doctrine of the soul, they believed in hell and heaven and the immortality of the soul. [149]

Giving so much importance to the immortality of the soul the ancient Filipino religion gave manifestations that our ancestors were animists.

The soul of the dead received the name "Nono" or "anito" and rarely pronouncing the name of God, they shortened their breaths in the spirit of the dead in their religion. [150]

We believed and proved that this was doubtless for they had a clear idea of a Supreme Being with some attributes of inferior gods which were the anitos. The opinion that the Filipinos were Polytheist was erroneous for they were, according to Paterno, similar to the saints of the Catholics.

D. THE COSMOS (THE UNIVERSE)

Our ancient people had the concept that Bathala was the creator of the universe and all things, that there were places for the dead, punishment, purification and glory for those who lived justly. Aside from paradise, there was also a Heaven for the Creator of the Universe. [151] These beliefs expressed the presence and intervention of God in the lives of our forebears. The nameless missionaries saw the miracles as Christian moral principles and loveliness gained relevance throughout the ages of our history. To support this Father Juan de San Francisco de San Antonio said, " that the tenets of Christianity was like the religion of the Filipinos in their beliefs of the purification of the souls in purgatory where souls were purified in the flames which would be extinguished someday.

All the different regions of the archipelago, regardless of geographical boundaries, were affected by the inevitable consequences of the time as recorded by the authors of antiquity. Although their beliefs were ancient ones of unrecorded times, they

[149] La Antigua Civilization Tagala by Paterno, page 148.
[150] This world could be admitted in various senses. It is considered synonymous to superstition.
[151] La Antigua Civilization Tagala by Paterno, page 39.

are still relevant to our time. A Christian belief in God was a spring of joy. It could hardly be said that there is no trace of this belief in us today or in this modern world. They had a special interest in philosophical reflection, particularly with regards to moral life and their fate after death. Could anybody deny that it is a precept of Hellenistic civilization that swept the world before the coming of Christ for the salvation of the world which was the purpose of the coming of Christ?[152]

Many authors had different interpretations; nevertheless, all concurred on our interpretations.

The following are the different summations of the authors of antiquity:

For the Tagalogs paradise was called Meca; a place of pain and affliction was called Casamaan. For the Visayans a place of enjoyment and contentment was called Olgan (Heaven); a place of pain was called Solad (Hell); a good of goodness called Sipada in whose care was the tree of human life[153]; two gods of evil known as Simuran and Siguinarugan; that when one dies he goes first down under the power of the spirit called Padaguita; he leaves for heaven by virtue of sacrifice and fiestas that were done by the Babaylanes.

E. MORALS

This period was pushed back with the audacious entrance of the Spaniards in to our beloved land. The Spaniards discovered the Oriental nobleness and virtue of the Filipino soul, tainted and adulterated by the Western influence. The Filipino knew a life of prosperity, laws, love and godliness. The unfolding of the soul left the discoverer on the shore of uncertainty that the hands of history could not help but reach out for him amongs the many and bends him to the metaphor of morality. All summarized in love and hospitality.

---

[152] Informe Sobre Filipinas by Mas, page 14.
[153] La Antigua Civilization Tagala by Paterno, page 143.

Love and hospitality abounded in their hearts. These Christian virtues manifested when in 1521, Magellan and his men arrived in the islands of Cebu. Too sick and tired to stand due to their long journey across the seas, the Spaniards were offered rooms to stay. Magellan refused the King of Cebu, explaining them it was not the customs of Spaniards to sleep on land while their ships were at sea. Food, wine, music and amiable friendship were for their asking. Likewise, when the expedition of Ruey Villalobos arrived in the islands of Samar, the Spaniards were given a royal welcome. Their ships on the shore were filled with water. The natives immediately emptied them and took care of the sick visitors. Sick men were transferred to private homes and given food and medicine at no cost. Cordiality, tenderness, care and brotherhood were bestowed on them and they wondered if heaven had led them to Christian paradise. These feelings of happiness and hospitality could be shared to the utmost of their being, if we look back and obtain a true knowledge of what has been through the hundred years leading to the Christianization of the Philippines.

Though it was not a dramatic scene, nonetheless it was an impressive one. The letters of the early missionaries gave us a glimpse thru the veil of the religiousness of our people and how Divine Providence played a role in the dream of the Christianization of the Filipino people.

In the Chronicle of the Orden de San Agustin, Father Grijalba narrated that upon the arrival of the expedition of Urdaneta in 1565 in Cebu, a well known lady, a niece of Tupas, together with other ladies eagerly begged to be baptized. "It was a marvelous thing that in a short item, they knew the Christian doctrine and we had no excuse to deny their baptism. The baptism was a great solemnity. The niece of Tupas brought a seven year old girl, a three year old boy and an eight girl."[154]

In 1596, Father Valerio Ledesma in his Chapters of Letters described in beautiful metaphors and personification the surprisingly rapid conversion of the inhabitants. "Everybody wanted to be

---

[154] Historia de las Islas Filipinas, by Juan Grijalva, Chapter XIII, p. 125.

baptized, even the rivers wanted to be baptized and you can hear no other in town, in houses, in their work and activities, except the singing of the Christian doctrines. Day and night, the children and the whole neighborhood joined together to sing and learn the doctrine."[155]

On October 5,1660, Father Gabriel Sanchez, a missionary in Bohol, said, "In three months more than a thousand souls were baptized; it gave me wonder and affection to see men come down the mountains to kneel and receive baptism. Young children, like angels from heaven, knew their prayers and we wondered who taught them. Even the native priests, called Catalonas, honestly craved for baptism."[156]

We believed that the Christianization of the Philippines was foreshadowed by the Greek culture long before the arrival of the Spaniards.

Though we lacked the primary records and the paucity of the secondary ones, the dramatic and impressive scene of the Christianization of the Philippines showed us an authenticity necessary to impress the intellectuals and opinion makers who will validate this work.

Our ancient civilization, as reflected in our culture and tradition of today, is inescapable evidence of the Hellenistic philosophy deeply embedded in the hearts of our people. Old and present adoption to environment and society completely subordinated these culture and traditions.

There are fundamental truths in life: it is a hypothesis that growth comes from things planted; that no man reaches a high degree in his station in life without the help of others; that man cannot reach his grandeur without the help of the Creator.

---

[155] Relacion de las Islas Filipinas, cap XXX36, page 80.
[156] Relacion Cap. LXX, page 155.

CIVILIZATION DEEPLY ROOTED HERE, PERFECT LOVE WAS EVERYWHERE

An authentic and unimpeachable culture that foreshadowed a Christian principle was the Filipino man's high view of woman. Religious records showed that Jesus was among those who took a low view of women; that a Jew would not greet a woman on the street, much less talk to her; a Jew blessed God that he was not born a gentile, a slave and a woman. It was impious for a Jew to discuss the law with women. Yet in all contacts recorded in the Gospel between Christ and the woman, there was nothing in Him that was not respectful and indeed sympathetic. [157]

Thus historians have come and gone but one pondering query has been shared: what was so strange in the Filipino soul that gave him a real notion of God, as affirmed by Paterno? The time was long ago before the Spaniards arrived and many things had happened before them but no creature had taken the sequence of events or facts, especially the coming of the sapient men from the Asian mainland whose records were unfolded by archeologists in the Philippines or if there was someone who could have destroyed it. Nevertheless, what these men could have brought represented the loftiest interest in human life. Summed up by many authors, a nameless religion and morality were entwined to become the foundation of our civilization and the unique tradition of the Philippines.

The amazing descriptions of authors about the social and political institutions analogous with those of the Graeco-Roman institutions excluded the possibility of coincidences and inconsistencies. The continuity of the undiluted Grecian had the absence of affinity. There it behooved us to believe that Divine Wisdom, through the coming of men from the Asian mainland, had showered His blessing or issued forth some droplets of mercy on these thousand isles. [158]

---

[157] Radiant Life by W. E. Sansgter, page 162.
[158] La Civilization Tagala by Paterno.

Records showed that the missionaries were excited for they found our ancient people on the path of righteousness – law abiding, peaceful and constructive citizens; therefore the principle of Christianity introduced by them were not strange ideas but enhances their already decent ideas. It showed the spoils of Divine Power in granting our ancient people all things that pertained to life of godliness, the full consciousness of the joy of life, the proper concept of the just and the unjust, the phenomenon of the universe, the power of God and above all, the price of heaven and the punishment of hell.

F. SUPERSTITIONS

Like the ancient Greeks and Romans, the ancient Filipinos, in their procrastinations and foretelling, predicted the future or discovered the future by observing certain natural signs.

Spanish authors described many narrations in this respect as follows. Father Collins explained, if the owl stopped or stayed on top of the roof at night, it meant death. Thus, people placed something on the rooftops of new houses to frighten the birds and ward off death in the homes, and there should be no reason for the house to be occupied. If someone happened on encounter a snake, he should discontinue his mission, no matter how important it was. If a person heard someone sneezed, if a mouse squeaked, a dog howled, the journey should be discontinued. The fisherman cannot have any on his first cast if he had a new net. No one should talk in the fisherman's house about his new net, nor about the newly bought dogs until they had caught and sorted their chances. Failure to observe such beliefs would remove the virtue of the new net and the expertness of the new dogs. A pregnant woman should not cut her hair for fear of losing her child.

Those walking on land should not talk about cases of the sea and those who were at sea should not take animals from the land without naming them. At the start of the navigation, one must swing the boat or ship with strands of rope, teeth of crocodiles, pangs of boars, for good luck.

According to Martinez de Zuniga if somebody was sick and in danger of death, he was offered rice, meat and wine to eat so he could get well, a practice still done today. There were beliefs like the patianac, which was said to impede the birth of the child due to its long tongue that supposedly reached the mother's uterus.

To avoid this the husband, entirely nude, barricaded the entrance to the house, lit a fire and furiously threw stones until they reached the wife. Another feared case was the ticbalang. It was a phantom that appeared in the form of an animal. Superstitions were contrary to religion.[159]

According to Father Delgado they called the crow Maylupa, which meant owner of the soil. Due to their fear of the crocodile, they called it Nono, which meant grandfather. With this they took some precautions and gave the crocodile something to eat. But Father Delgado felt that in their superstition and prognostication, the early Filipinos did not recognize any deity or divinity in those animals or evil spirits; although due to fear, they made sacrificial offerings such as food. They were afraid of trees because they believed that a ghost would appear through them. Hence, they were afraid to cut down trees , fearing some sickness or misfortune would fall on them. In the houses of fishermen and hunters it was bad luck to talk about fish, dogs and new tools used in their business.

Many times they never named their proper instruments for their navigation but used other names to signify it as in sail which is layag.[160]

---

[159] Historia de las Islas Filipinas by Zuniga, page 36.
[160] Historia de Filipinas by Delgado, page 363.

G. SACRIFICE

Unlike the pagan nations, the Philippines never sacrificed human beings.

The type of sacrifice depended on their intentions. If it was for display, they called it Feast of the Great God. People gathered together in the Chief's house which was adorned with Moorish-style cloth. There the visitors gathered as they struck the sacrificial animal. They danced, and divided the animal among themselves, and feasted on it with reverence as if it was blessed bread.

If the feast was for thanksgiving for the recovery of the sick, the priest ordered a new house to be constructed at the expense of the sick. Construction was completed in a short time because of the abundance of materials. They transferred the sick to the new house and killed an animal for the feast. The priest anointed the sick with the blood of the sacrificial animal. The priest watched the animal with an open mouth as a soothsayer would. Moving backward she tried to chase the animal away with a wry face and with hands and feet threw foam from his mouth as if to enchant. Turning back, he prophesied for the sick. If the prophesy was for death, the priest saluted the sick, praised him and informed him that he was selected by their ancestors to join them in the next life. He sent his regards to his ancestors through the sick man. Through flatteries and lies, he induced the sick to accept death. Fasting continued and the sick from then on was considered an "anito" (spirit).

Due to the harsh weather changes brought on by monsoon rains and the natural shifts of land, records were destroyed after three and half centuries and the detailed account of our way of life remained a secret. But now and then we come across the writings of historians and so we get a little glimpse of our past. The Chinese writers who came to the Philippines before the Spaniards had nothing but praises for our father's high morals and decent life as compiled by the author Paterno.

H. TEMPLES

Many authors disclaimed the existence of temples in pre-Spanish Philippines. However, the temple ruins, details and awesome descriptions by many authors lead us to conclude that temples did exist. Those who misunderstood the doctrine of Bathalanism referred to the temples as caves; nevertheless, they greatly admired their beauty while doubting their existence. Were the temples there by mere chance or were they the aftermath of chaos?

Their god, Bathala, although believed to be omnipotent, was enthroned on an altar and enclosed, free from the touch of the petitioning humanity. Altars, built on rocks in mountains without pictures or image, representative of his Divinity, were great and majestic in form. They believed that neither the form of a woman nor the sun would do him justice. A simple line of the rays of the Divine light represented the sublime, invisible, impalpable, and spiritual.

Those who did not understand the Bathalanism called the temples caves, though they were filled with admiration of the costly and grandiose work that seemed to speak.[161]

Sinibaldo vividly described one of the ruins of a temple northeast of San Mateo, an hour walk from the barrio of Malate. It consisted of two big mountain rocks, Paminitas and Sablayan, whose edges opened to a path leading towards the branch of a big river. The mountain on the left side had a cave whose opening faced south. The mountain stood 100 yards from the river filed with trellises (lattice) formed in an arch, giving a beautiful view of the splendor of the sun. The stone was entirely of marble on which a high wall stood in the form of an arch. Underneath was a cavity in the form of a small chapel.[162]

---

[161] La Antigua Civilization Tagala by Paterno, page 84.
[162] Ibid.

I. PRIEST

The Tagalogs' priests had ancient names such as the Sonat, the Catalonas and the Panggataon.

According to Father Juan San Francisco de San Antonio the Sonat was the bishop among the ancient priests. Much revered he pardoned and condemned sins and ordained priests. Ministry was common in the islands. The Honorable and principled walkec among them and were held in great esteem. Some believed tha the Sonat was the teacher of some of the honest excorcists of the times. They believed that the Sonat's office was from Borneo.[163]

The Catalonas, whose office was not considered an honorable one, collected the gifts during the sacrifice.

The Paggataon foretold and prognosticated the future of the archipelago.

---

[163] La Civilization Tagala by Paterno, page 93.

Chapter V

CULTURE

Culture measures the elements of millions of years of evolutionary changes of men's far reaching success in their respective endeavors. Men tempered and refined the physical matter produced by nature that has long been before us.

From the embryonic stage of prehistory the cultural evolution of humanity were distinguished according to the predominance of the materials they utilized in their aspirations, the utensils and arms of the people.

The Age of Wood cut, carved and polished. The Age of Bronze and the Age of Iron were characterized by the advance of its peculiar economic forms in its cultural evolution.

W. Schmidt compared the different cultural cycles. He showed the existence of three diverse groups in a series of cultural cycles. The first cycle was called the archaic or primitive cycle, followed by the primary and the secondary cycles.

According to W. Schmidt the primitive belonged to a collective group who did not cooperate with nature for production and instead depended on the spontaneous production. People in the primary group encouraged production and the third group were people who fused the various cycles.

Schmidt described them as follows:

Localizing the cultural cycles, it was observed that these people called primitive could be found in the extreme regions of the continent, in the islands or places that were not accessible to all humanity, that seeing a superior culture, they took refuge in remote places except some who absorbed the new culture were separated in great distance that never had any communication for millions of years.

Schmidt further divided the primitive cycles into four groups:

a) Central cycles – to this group belonged to the Negritos of Central Africa, the Vedas of Ceylon, the Semang of Mallaca, the Negritos of the Philippines and those of Celebes. People of the Central cycles were the first group of the primitive cycles; they seemed to be the most ancient and they had a nomadic life. They had no knowledge of agriculture and ranching. They lived in huts or houses poorly built, covered with grass and twigs of trees, they used fire, arms, wood and bones which made them the most antique in pre-historic times.

b) Austral cycles – represented the Bosquiman of South Africa, the Tamils, the Kurnes of Southeast of Australia and the pygmies of South America.

c) Arctic cycle – embraced the primitive people of northeast Asia and North America up to the Hudson Bay.

d) Transition culture – They were found principally in Australia near the ocean, in the regions of the upper Nile, the Meridional Sudan and in old California and Mexico.[164]

In the past people of the primitive stage were considered in the stage of barbarism. It was a stage of decay and degradation compared to other well developed and civilized cultures.

The account on the general evolution, as observed among the people of Asia who had an influence on the Philippines, could confirm that the territories like China, India, Madagascar, Celebes and other countries of the world experienced the process of barbarism in the remote past. But this stage, burdened not only by their struggle for food, clothing, decoration, arms and defenses but also by other necessities like the preservation of life and properties, developed immensely to the extent that they dominated nature. They showed cultural resources in their invention and the patient work of their people.

---

[164] Historia de los Rigiones by Jesus Enciso, page 11.

With the march of time, the inventive spirit of men produced a paulatinian stage in the various cultural stages. [165]

It is generally said that cultural matters diffuse more than spiritual matters, but contrary examples with events and myths, and the major tenacity demonstrated that elements do not pass from hand to hand nor from mouth to mouth. They were very much interlaced with the internal structure of society. Examples of this were the religious organizations, conveniences, power, decoration and liquor which were more diffused and found no contradiction.

---

[165] Humanity does not progress in all times, nor degenerate, and this is understood not to be among people whose culture were inconsistently united, but with some cultural elements, confronted in the same group of people. The dominion of nature formed the extreme intellectual and exterior social life and the economic swells, that lapsed from one town to another and to other.... followed by degration. But the intimate quality of social life, the graciousness of characters, the adherence to family and the departure from the exaltation of the spirits, had not resulted in a favorable advance, but had developed in egotism and vice.

Chapter VI

AGRICULTURE, INDUSTRY AND COMMERCE

This chapter is of singular importance, a measure of the highest order that marked the evolutionary changes of men's for reaching succes in their endeavors in the past centuries. Men had tempered and refined the physical matter produced by nature that had been before us.

From the embryonic stage of history the cultural evolution of humanity was distinguished according to the predominance of the materials men utilized in their aspirations: the utensils or implements used in their farms, the tools necessary for their trade and the manufacture of their arms.

The Age of Wood used cut, carved or polished; the Age of Bronze and the age of Iron were all characterized by their advance of the peculiar forms in the historic cultural evolution.

In these school of cultural cycle author W. Schmidt showed the existence of three groups of cultural cycles, two of which – the primary and secondary – were collectors of nature's products.

We understand that such united cultural elements (arts, science, economic systems, social organizations, industry and religion) constantly appear associated in the territories to all normal forms of human activities.

A. COMMERCE

There is abundant data about the commerce enjoyed by the Philippine archipelago on the arrival of the Spaniards. Like the civilized nations of the time, the Philippines effectively used money and barter-trade.

Money, the life blood of every civilized nation, is the principal tool that provides a convenient method by which goods and service may be indirectly exchanged. It did not have to be a

Embroidery in the Philippines

Winnowing rice.

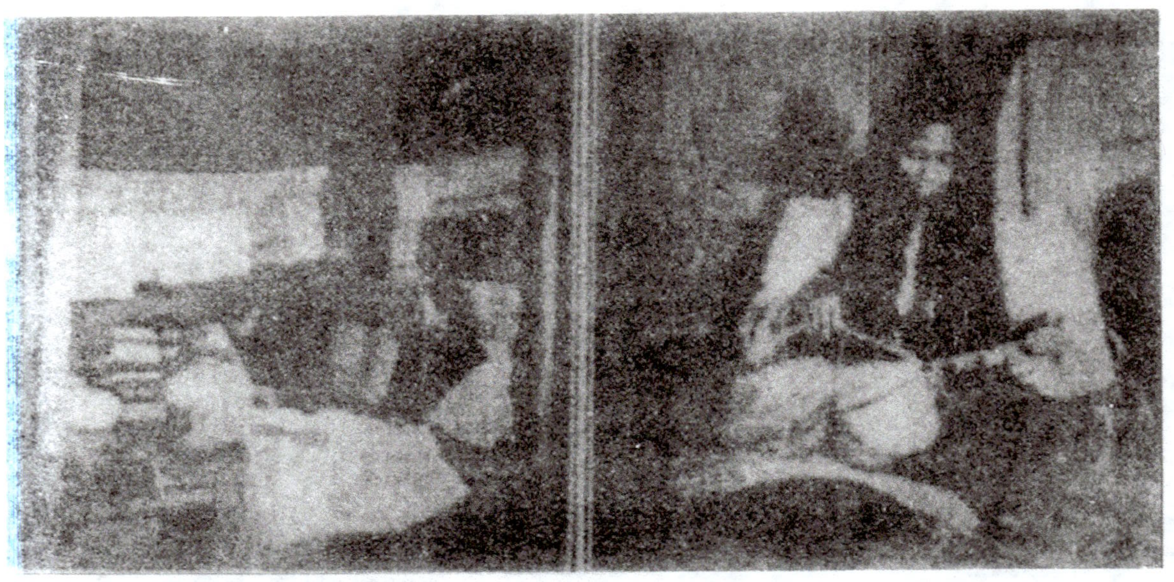

Retail selling of dry goods.

Hat weaving

Preparing clay for making pottery.

specific thing, as long as it was accepted generally. It may be a form of commodity or any piece of paper. Under the barter system, or direct exchange, as practiced by the primitive people, the value of the trade was very narrowly restricted. [166]

By the above simple philosophy of money, we can compare the following description of Mas about our ancient people's experience in their commerce and how they beautifully harmonized.

They engaged in commerce through barter, although they also used gold in their buying and selling. They did not have money as we have today. Instead they used powdered gold which were weighed in balance like our "Talero". [167]

The major weight was called Tael whose value was equal to ten reals of the Spanish silver coins. The Tael was divided into two Tingas; the Tingas divided into two Sapaha; the Sapaha into various Sangsaga.

Their abacus was a mound of little stones with special names which indicated the summary increase. A baul or box was used to measure cereals and other things which had an equivalent value of a cavan or grain of a hundred weight. [168]

A cavan contained twenty-four gantas and a ganta consisted of eight chupas.

To measure dimensions, they used dipa, a measure of six feet; a dankal which was a measure of one palm; a timuro which was the distance between the end of a thumb to the end of the forefinger; one damac was the length of the five fingers in one hand; the sansale was the length of one finger.

---

[166] With respect to the Tagalogs, Morga wrote, "The Tagalogs were dedicated to commerce and their common business was barter of domesticated animals and slaves and in the prevailing prices, they used to pay gold." Sucesos by Morga Cap. VIII for 144.

[167] Description about the existence of this topic should be read in the epoch of the Visayan conquest by Isabelo de los Reyes, page 36 y ss.

[168] Pigafetta said about the Filipinos:" These people were lovers of justice. They had weights and measure; their balance was made of wood hanging in the middle of a cord, one side had a small plate suspended with three little cord, on the other side the weight of the metal was equal to the weight of the small plate, the weight is added which is equivalent to the pounds etc. and the object is then weighed." Primer Viaje Intorno al Globo, page 79-80.

They counted their harvest with the moons, referring to periods past the first harvest to the second harvest. The year was called taon which were joined moons. The days were called araw.

The commercial cities were Jolo, Manila and Butuan. Commercial life was well advanced in Luzon as well as in the Visayas. They knew confiscation, exchanges, guarantee and compound interest.

The authors differently determined the value of those Philippine money from the 125 pesetas of Mas; according to Morga a Tael was equal to 40 pesetas. According to Fr. J.F. San Antonio, 10 reals of silver was 250 pesetas ; to Malliat 6 pesos or 30 pesetas.

They also knew the changes of the season and gave them names. They knew the hours of the day by the crowing of the cock and by the position of the sun and its shadows. By means of the words of those elusive objects they understood the domestic and public occurrences.

In commerce, Mas said, "They knew the payments of installments; the guarantor, beneficial lending and interest of the interest. Through usury the poor and the unfortunate became the slaves of the rich."

"If the operations of exchanges were ineffective in their own towns or territory, they crossed the sea to transact with other islanders."[169]

Based on this information, it can be concluded in the words of Santa Ines: as the nature of behaviour was to join the best, the Philippines had participated with the best qualities as it was the end and the center of the Occidental and Oriental Indies, coming and navigating from one place to another. Thus the Philippines had participated in the best and advantageous commerce.

For these reasons a country found to have a continuous relationship with other Asiatic civilization could not permanently remain passive to various influences and be found in a state of barbarism but instead join in civilization.

---

[169] Historia de las Islas Filipinas by Father Santa Ines, page 39.

Luck, indeed, is light from heaven
Not to all mortals are given.
T' is a blessing in disguise
T' is done history testifies.

B. INDUSTRY

Industry is an enduring reality developed by men. It has its foundation in the minds of men and moved them to the greatest discoveries they needed for their survival in order to fight the absurdities inherent in life.

According to the records of antiquity their habitual precision and speed helped our people enjoy the components of progress in peace, joy, wisdom, grace and contentment. This situation belonged to their epoch and geographical period, many centuries ago; yet our modern commercialism pales into insignificance compared to the social orders, peace and morality enjoyed by our forefathers. For centuries our forefathers received a jaundice look from authors who failed to discern the varied interpretations of their beautiful culture, in the face of the amazing traits and progress of our people.

Industry recognizes the ingenuity of people. It provides the substantial evidence and ground for people's worth, the solid and the unimpeachable basis of our ancient civilization.

These negative authors must have been unwilling to accept the reality that the Philippine archipelago in the field of industry was in a considerable stage of advancement as shown by their industrial development. In the field of artisans they had wood for the construction of their houses, ships and boats which they had developed in great perfection.

This chapter is of singular importance, a measure of the highest order that marked the evolution of men's far reaching success in their endeavors in the past centuries. They had tempered and refined the physical matters produced by nature that had lain before us. A living example of their ingenuity is the Banawe Rice Terraces in Banawe Mt. Prov. considered one of the wonders of the world and stairway to the sky. It is measured from end to end, the terraces would stretch a total length of 22,400 kilometers.

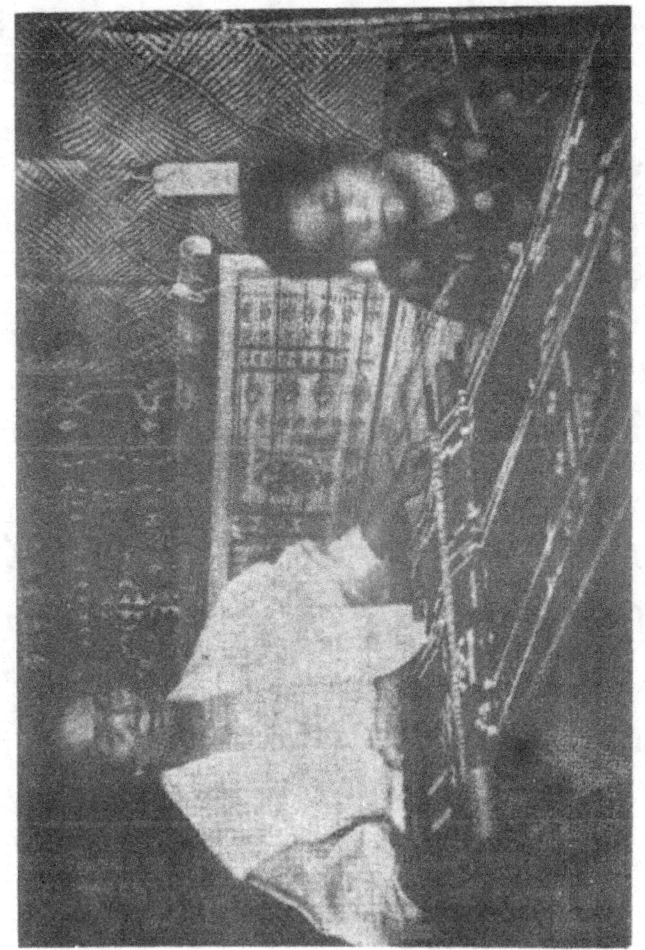

Cloth weaving antedates history

The most important manifestation of the industry of the Philippine archipelago on the arrival of the Spaniards was in the field of Industrial Textile found to be advance in the Artesan stage— the construction of houses and ships which were in great perfection; beat[170C] bark or skin or rinds of many things to make dresses; to make tiles; dyed cotton, made beautiful mats, built houses adopted to théir climate, made fine jewelries from gold and silver. They also worked in iron, copper and tin.

They also exploited minerals, particularly gold. They made beautiful articles for decorations, arms, boats and ships.

Father F. de San Antonio describe the arms of our ancient forefathers: spears, bows and arrows whose points were toasted in fire, broad swords, big and fine knives, hard embers of wood, breast plates of reed or canes.

Aside from the arms enumerated the Spaniards found cannons in Manila and Tondo and cast in on or melting of artilleries. These were found by the Muslims who were directly or indirectly influenced by the Arabs.[171]

With respect to their ship building industries, they turned sturdy wood vessels propelled by sails or oarsmen and they had international trade with Japan and other countries on the Asian mainland and the archipelago to the South. [172] Moraga commended on these ships, "There were many native teachers who could make any kind of ship in the Island."

C. NOURISHMENT

Food is an important necessity to which men dedicate their first efforts. The navigators who accompanied Magellan were the first Europeans who gave news to the outside world of the abundance of food in the Philippine islands. After four months of ocean

[170C] San Antonio, Morga – Ibid, Susesos page 28.+
[171] Manila Times page 12 "Our Usable and Ancient Past"
[172] Bark of two trees were stripped and later spunned into rough threads and then woven.

voyage, the European's shortage of food and provisions ended after they landed in the islands of Cebu.[173]

People in the rudimentary stage, immediately resolved their food problem with nature's help without exerting a lot of efforts. Plants from the meadows and animals from the mountains and from the sea were in great abundance.

In terms of food, M. Haberlandt interestingly determined the customs and manner of cooking, eating and drinking. The Bosquiman stood on his feet, and threw water in his mouth with his right hand; the Incas of Malaca drank from rolled leaves; but the Philippines by the time of the arrival of the Spaniards, had already passed this stage. The narrations of Pigafetta served as example; referring to the time they were in the palace of the King of Cebu, he said the Captain's deputy and the interpreter were served breakfast of many meats served on porcelain plates and glasses.

Other authors narrated that for their ordinary sustenance they had clean, polished rice which were cooked in water, called in Spanish "morisqueta"; the viand were classes of fish abundant in many places; cooked with water and salt whose broth gave flavor to the rice. In parties they added venison, beef and salted pork. Food was served on plates placed on low square tables or round ones without table cloth and napkins. People ate around the tables.

No one would ever make the mistake of putting his or her hand on the plates containing the viands, nor drink in a glass already used by someone. It was not necessary to ponder on elements that were important in the daily lives of our people, when the Spaniards arrived. Wine, sugar and salt were in hand.

Among the wines most common were the wines from palms called Quilang which was sweet like that of India; the Tuba, a wine of the Visayan which came from rice.

---

[173] Aganduru described how the Filipinos met the Spaniards: With jackets they came to sell chickens, rice, fruits and pork which were in abundance. Some came bringing food and drink to our sick and weak soldiers. They felt that they had entered paradise after their hunger and hardships. "Documentos Inedito para las Historia de Spana page 44.

Primitive way of cooking

It was observed that the state of the alimentation of our people were equal with other nations as deduced from the narration of F. Collin ..."wheat from China, flour from Japan and India came and ordinarily there was no lack of food."

Meat was abundant. Wild pigs were substituted for mutton. Domestic pigs were raised under the houses as done by the natives of other nations. The Chinese raised cocks, hens, capons and sold various mountain birds at reasonable prices. Native fruits were preserved admired and sold to India, Oriental countries and Mexico.[174]

Father Joaquin de Zuniga described the abundance of food: "Rice was the principal product which they cultivated before the arrival of the Spaniards. They also had some vegetables like patani, mongo, firijoles meso etc.

They raised chickens, carabaos, goats, doves and other birds. The young shoots of the Bejoco and other plants were used as food and so it was not necessary to work.

With these cases it was known that there were groups that depended on the nature's reserve and therefore some believed this was evidence of a barbaric stage. However, it was not a sign of barbarism but a sign of abundance.

D. CLOTHING

One of the elements of life is clothing. Each nation has its own style of clothing according to its climate and the influence of the foreign countries in contact with her. The Philippines, being a tropical country, has a style that distinctly differed from the Europeans and other cold countries.

Logically each country have a style convenient for her. Thus countries with cold climate have to use color and thick clothing, while tropical one like the Philippines had to use light colors, sheer and as minimal as possible materials. These elements play an

---

[174] Historia de las Islas Filipinas M. de Aganduru page 37 y ss.

Tipos Indios-Bisayas

important role that ought to be considered as a sign of intelligence. The different clothing styles reflected the practicality of people.

Hence, it is an intellectual challenge to understand why the different modes of dressing make sense in civilization. It is an emotional challenge, for what one thinks proper and natural for him is doubtful or queer for another. It is nobody's business except the wearer, yet much criticism was given to the dressing styles of our forefathers, taking one for a whole.

Engross concern for truths
T'is the sweetest thing on earth
Let it rule thy heart.
T'is something free
And feel no constrain in thy heart

While some authors side-tracked truth, nevertheless some had given us inspirations with nuggets of truth. That if our forefathers had a different psychology of clothing, perhaps we could deduce that they substituted the psychology in gold.

Like the Greeks, they used mats from palms and hats of felts. The Tagalogs used hats from palm leaves which they called Salacot. From petioles they obtained fibers for hats, baskets and cases of cigars. The luxurious items they had were symbolic figures of precious metals.

Inspite of their psychological costumes in dresses, they had commendable personalities and modern appearances of prosperity and self-reliance. They had appropriate dresses for parties, church and for work. We had searched all the magic keys that would unlock the door of our covered patrimonial wealth.

In parties and fiestas, Chiefs and other officials used formal floor-length skirts, black, long sleeve shirts adjusted to the wrists, which they called Barong mahaba, comparable to our present Barong Tagalog, a decent and respectable man's shirt. For the field work, they used ordinary long dresses made of cloth for their protection from the sun. Their holiday dresses were embroided materials of silk and gold.

The old Filipino dress with the saya, the scarf,
skirt and cinamay sleeves

Tagalog dress of Luzon

What our ancient people lacked in clothing they made up in gold which were abundant to cover the whole body. They even knew how to match their clothes with beautiful colors.

A woman's dress consisted of a waist length blouse where a nicely colored square scarf was securely wrapped around the waist. This was called **Tapis.**

This Tapis was strictly used by the inhabitants and were usually of silk. The women used **Saya**, a long skirt where the Tapis was used over it, on special occasion. While in the house, the woman only used **Saya** without the Tapis.

They also used a cloth called cobija which was head to foot covering, in the style of Spanish Mantilla.

They used gold to cover their bodies, ears, throats, wrists, fingers and legs. They wore silk slippers embroidered in gold. Few used shoes. Older women were partial to long gowns which gave them an aura of respectability.

The men's garments were composed of short, thigh-length jackets, similar to the Americans and the Chineleans and short salawal or pantalon that hardly covered the knees, not opened in front but on the sides where cords could be found; a covered cloth that covered the thighs, which covered all the buttocks and knees, then back to back between the knees. The chiefs added three ornaments of cloth without buttons that reached the feet, and black sleeves adjusted to the wrists. These were used in ceremonies.

The chiefs and priests used caps in the summer, like those used by the Greeks and Buddhists.

The general rule was to use a colored band under the arm; long narrow strips of cloth adorned the heads in the form of a turban which they called *Pautong*.

The sleeves hung openly on the shoulders. Colored Pautong were used by persons of rank: Those who killed enemies used red Pautong on which they listed the names of seven enemies they had killed.

The inhabitants of Central Luzon, Abra and the Ilocos regions called Tingians wore skirts and trousers like the Chinese. The men used turbans on their heads, women used skirts and blouses which were opened in front.

They were generally clean, curious and lived in tribes of submissive and peaceful people.

E. DWELLING

The brilliant John Ruskin has said, "There is no wealth but life". All conjunctive elements used by men to satisfy the necessities of his life and dreams are the protection of life from fierce animals and influence of bad weather etc. This protection of life could measure or judge the cultural stage of its users.

Indeed so wrong were those who gave our ancient people a bunch of negations, when on the contrary, ancient authors gave distinct impressions that our ancient people gravitated to the top of their understanding like any of the civilized nation of the time. Dwelling is the sum total of all, for without the protection of life, the overabundance offered by Nature is of naught.

Our quest, therefore, at this stage resolve itself into a dual task. First, to see with clarity the aspects and purpose of the dwellings of the primitive people or people attached to nature; and secondly people who mastered nature and developed them were cultured people.

The primitive people constructed simple houses principally as a resting place at night and abandoned it during the day. The Negrito abandoned his hut of clay and with his cloth of animal skin wandered in the forest. The necessity of sleep for a primitive man was decisive. On the other hand, the civilized man dominated this necessity by limiting some hours for work and recreation.

The Australian Negros, the Paupans, and the Menesans usually dedicated their major time to sleep, like what Tacito described with the ancient Germans. [175]

---

[175] Ethnographia page 67 by M. Habrelandt.

The Filipinos demonstrated their aptitude in the construction of their dwellings and utilizing materials that were on hand. Like civilized people, those who were in stable political and economic situation built better houses not only for protection but also for the immediate physical comfort and mental satisfaction. They also built special houses for fiestas and celebrations.

The common houses were made of palm leaves fastened with thin weed (bejoco) and were very adaptable to the usually hot climate. The affluent ones constructed their houses with wood frame and roofed also with palm leaves. The ancient constructions of our forefathers were not different from our constructions now, but for their use of bejoco as their nails.

As civilized people they knew the philosophy of good homes as a rudimentary of healthy living. Authors described how they never placed wood floors close together. Instead they spaced them leaving holes to let the wind pass through it for ventilation, since the country is in the torrid zone. Out of palm leaves they made their windows and partitions for rooms which were necessary for the service needed.[176]

In solemn occasions, they extended their houses with branches of trees and decorations.

In one of the parties they called "Pandot", which usually lasted four days, they adored their anitos with their friends.

Nothing could be more practical than the way our ancient people showed their aptitude in their cleanliness. A basin or a container of water was placed at the foot of the stairs... by rubbing the feet against each other the water easily fell on the bamboo or palm floor on the foot of the stairs. They washed their feet before they entered the house, especially during the rainy season.[177]

---

[176] Historia de las Islas Filipinas' page 20 by M. Zuniga
[177] Opinion cited F. Collin page 62 y ss.

This is not the only example of the Filipino cleanliness. As said by F. Collin: "All the islanders, for their extreme inclination to bathe, they preferred to live on the banks of rivers, for the nearer to the water the better."

They observed the rule of cleanliness as they bathed any hour of the day. A newly born infant was submerged in water. The mother held the baby in a sitting position, with water reaching the throat or neck.

Ordinarily, bathing times were at sunrise and after their work, as if they were born in water, women swam like fishes.

Hundred Islands, Pangasinan

Chapter VII

SOCIAL HABITS, MUSIC AND DANCES

To reach the end of these three homogenous topics, we have combined them into one Chapter.

On the arrival of the first expedition of the Spaniards, the Spanish historians first observed the tranquility, the beautiful life of the inhabitants of the land, the courtesies and the education of its people, the human life they enriched and maintained.

These feats showed that our civilization pre-dated the arrival of the Spaniards. They saw a seed out of which civilization developed shown in their hearts and mind. They saw that the Philippines was one of an interesting dynamic region of the world, and a profile of attractions. Many authors assumed that there must have been an event that transpired, that there must be something to explain the seemingly wireless movement that gave the Philippines this miraculous phenomenon.

Has it ever occurred to us what must have been the power that caused the Philippines to be the only Catholic nation in the Orient?

From the beginning of our work we presumed the Greek culture as our pivotal point on which our ancient civilization rested; that the Greek was the first culture in the hearts and minds of our ancient people. Through the principle of the maxim "first impression is lasting", could apply to our hypothesis for our tradition and culture are demonstrated factor which transcended all mis-conceptions, mystical people, etc. described by man-made book of fiction.

This Greek culture gave the Filipino people a faith that became their heritage. They saw that portion of the Universe where no humans have seen but guided by love for a human soul; we considered our case as one of the unanswerable mysteries of God's work.

It is exceedingly a rare quality to see a person doing the right thing without being told to do so.

We need only to read the letters and annals of the early missionaries and historians to pierce the veil of maturity and growth of our civilization, especially on morals and courtesy.

The first who took note was Father Chirino when he said, "The Filipinos, particularly the Tagalogs, were not like the Chinese and Japanese in their actions (ceremonious) which were in words and actions; our ancestors were civil, polite, and courteous. They uncovered their heads upon encountering, not because they had hats but because they wore a Potong, a neckerchief-like, on their heads.

Father Collins had this comment, "The Filipinos particularly the Tagalogs had limitations in their talking and writings, that showed they were like people of polite nations. They never say you in the second and third person singular or plural, but always in the third person, particularly woman to man although they were equal; never were treated less than a senior or sir, or my lord. They wrote fine and excellent courteous letters.

When one of an inferior rank spoke to a superior, he showed courtesy by a low inclination of the head, raising both hands joined on the cheeks, raised a foot in the air, and in doing this it was to stand doubling the knees without reaching the floor, leaving the body with the face up. In this position he removed his Potong, stayed aside waiting to be asked, because to talk first before a question was asked was considered bad manners."

Equally, Paterno recorded - no person can pass without asking permission and while passing the body was deeply inclined.

Another courtesy among the Tagalogs was by putting some syllables before the name as Aling Maria; if a man, it was Mang Pedro. The respect of children to parents was venerable like the Hebrews to their Gods.

To strangers the name of the husband was pronounced with the name of the son before it, as "father of Juan".

For those who had no children, neighbors and friends were invited to join together to adopt a name for him which was called Pamagat that was usually a prefrasi or metaphor; or one suitable for him; if he were strong and sturdy he was called Bacal or iron or Diamtashan or cannot be spent.

Aganduru described Filipino hospitality: "The king of Cebu offered Magellan a pilot to guide him to the Molucas and some necessities for his army. Equally he offered rooms for his soldiers who were angry about the long trip. But Magellan said that it was not the custom of the Spaniards to leave their ships at night and sleep on land... there was so much friendship that in their conversation they were very civil and polite."[178]

Pigaffeta described our hospitality; "When we went to the land, whether night or day, we were invited to eat and drink and with their cooked food we drank their wine in glasses. Ordinarily we spent five or six hours at the tables."[179]

Aganduru described on the arrival of the Spaniards the expedition of Ruy de Villalobos: "Not knowing where they were after a storm in the Island of Ibao, now Samar, the Indios with charity and love came as if they were in a Christian land. The Indios emptied their ships which were filled with water. They carried the soldiers who could not stand due to hunger. They cured the sick with their medicinal herbs free of charge.

The tradition for this fine culture according to records goes back thousands of years before the coming of the Spaniards and stood like the hills, today nothing has been changed and effaced.

MATRIMONY

We just referred this to the social aspects of matrimony and popular customs for the motive it produced.[180]

---

[178] Collin Labor Evangelica page 58 y ss.

[179] Historia de Filipinas by Aganduru page 44.

[180] This custom was scrupulously observed by the Persians, among the slaves and their master and with kings. This was still observed by the Tagalogs. Opinion cited by Paterno page 301

A. ENGAGEMENT AND BETHROTAL

Before entering the house of the sweetheart, the lover made three taps on the steps of the stairs, although he was being seen by someone in the house, he called, "Tao po" to a person in the house.

He would not go up the house unless someone answered, "tuloy po kayo" or enter, permission was only given up to the stairs. Luckily it gave him the permit to enter the house "tuloy po kayo," or Enter, Sir.

In this case the lover takes two or three steps until he hears those in the house say, "tuloy po cayo." Enter, Sir.

The owner of the house might be fixing something or preparing himself to receive the visitor, before the visitor was answered.

Without looking around he was instructed to a chair and receiving table; and remained standing until invited to "umupo kayo." Sit down, Sir.

It was a rule to sit straight without moving the hands joined together, eyes cast towards the floor and the hands placed in the mouth like the customs of the Persian. This was a sign of fine education testimony of respect and humility.

The personality and virginity of a woman (dalaga) cannot be a pawn to the impure spirits of man.

The maximum visit did not exceed one hour (there must be no abuse with the pain of being considered high-spirited and discourteous, a quality rejected by the ladies who loved the Bagong tao (single man) who possess humility and quietness.

In the narration of Mas he said, "We have never seen or observed any sprightliness and boldness even in a woman of ill refute for they feigned and conquered.

During those visits, the lady was always accompanied by the mother or any member of the family. Hardly could the suitor talk to the lady.

The Filipino woman had the "Victorian beauty" (where the emotion was always submerged beneath the facade of rational men.)

It was said that this was the urbanity of the Filipina woman. In Manila and any indication of calling a man in the street or from a window, as was practiced in Europe, could be considered objectionable and the woman could be arrested by the police.

B. MARRIAGE CEREMONY

Marriage ceremony in the Philippines is of much importance. The height of the ceremony is in the wedding day.

Two committees were formed, one from the group of the bride which consisted of witnesses, friends, relatives, parents, and slaves presented with a band of music. The groom's group consisted of his relatives and friends and guided by the Ama sa Ligao. (or sponsors)

Both committees proceeded to the house of the Sonat or priest. Mass said that the groups marched slowly, especially the sponsors, accompanied by slaves with a parasol of silk to protect them from the heat of the sun and from the rain. Old men stayed behind followed by slaves and other servants.

The Sonat united the hands of the contracting parties and after invoking the sacred name of Bathala, drew a little amount of blood from both with a sacred pin. The bride and groom were served on one plate and drunk water from the same glass with the blood in the glass. While performing the function, the priest invoked the sacred name of Bathala and asked the contracting parties, if they loved each other. The question was asked two times with the answer– "I do." They again were asked to eat in the same plate and drink from the same glass.

As practice today they also used cords and veils. The priest then said," you are witness to the union."

This scene was called "paghaharap" a feast day that was repeated the next day.

The helpers extended the feast by music and fireworks illuminating the palapala. With food, songs and dances the feast lasted from seven to fifteen days. During these feasts the newly weds were never seen alone for each one went with the groups of their friends.

Like our modern weddings, friends and relatives gave donations to help the cost of the ceremonies.

C. MUSIC AND DANCES

It is always said that "Music is the language of the soul." As Shakespeare said," Rare is the man who has no music in his soul."

Music is from the Greek word "mousike" – "the science of the art of pleasing; expressive or intelligent combination of tones; the making of such combinations into special and definite significant to harmony and rythm".[181]

Music and dances are artistic manifestations that are compactly united. Music spontaneously stimulated dances which had its own music from the beginning.

Music is co-natural or in-born in man. From the beginning man made musical instruments; with his voice he expressed his love,compassion, fancy and concerns; with his hands he felt happiness and anger; and with his feet he stamped the floor.

The human voice first launched a cultural song inspired by happiness, anger or hunger. Man's palms served to accompany the acts and was the first rudimentary stage when musical instruments were still unknown.

The Philippines, pictured as uncivilized and barbaric or delayed in civilization, had many musical instruments before the arrival of the Spaniards. The Kudyapa, the most artistic of their instruments, had two strings of wire strung with a plume.[182] It symbolized poetry in the Philippines, like the lyre of classical Greece and Rome.[183] According to Father Chirino the Filipinos played this with liveliness and dexterity and appeared to get their human voices from this metallic strings.[184]

---

[181] Opinion cited by M. Haberlandt, page 145.
[182] Opinion cited by F. Collin, page 37.
[183] Opinion cited by G. Zaide, page 83
[184] Opinion cited by Father Chirino, page 39.

The Bangui, another instrument, had a style similar to that of the flute. Its sound was very sad and seemed to emanate from a tomb.

The Kalalang was a nasal flute used by the mountain people.

Zaide cited other instruments such as the Gong of the Igorrots, the Bombo of the Visayans, the Kulintang of the Morros and the Torotot of the Tagalogs.

Father Collin wrote about the graceful dance called the Kumintang.

The Visayans, Zimbals and Bicolanos had war-like dances using spears, bells and other arms just as the Trojan and the Greeks did. It was common practice to dance to the ringing of bells and noisy clangs of hollow metals. They had a beautiful dance with actions of various styles, slow and fast steps, wriggling bodies coming together and then withdrawing. It was like the dance of astronomers but it had grace and gentility.

In addition to the Kumintang of the Tagalogs, the Ilocanos had the Kinoton; the Tingians had the Tadek and the Bicolanos had the Salampati.

D. FUNERAL CUSTOMS

Our ancestors had incredible funeral customs as described by Father Collin, "After the death of a sick person, the family and relatives of the deceased cried and wailed and even hired professional criers during the wake. Like psalm readers during Passion Week, the criers recounted the laudable deeds and the blunders of the deceased during his lifetime. The body was washed and fumigated before it received perfumes from different natural ingredients; others were smoked with gums from mountain trees. The rich and the powerful were embalmed with liquors and aromatic spirits in the manner of the Hebrews to prevent corruption. They also used Beetle nut, made famous in India. They threw a big quantity of beetle nut juice inside the deceased's mouth.

The poor's sepulchres were in the underground holes of their houses. After three days of mourning, the rich and the powerful were placed in an indestructible coffin adorned with jewels and laminated with gold. Gold were placed in the eyes and mouth of the dead. The coffin was wrapped in a roll of cloth and placed in a concave trunk of wood; well covered and fitted so that no insects could penetrate. With diligence, and preparation no body decomposed. This coffin was usually placed in one of three places selected by the deceased when he was alive; or in a place among the jewels usually guarded on the raised floors, which were opened in a pit and closed surrounded with windows but not covered with earth. Together with the coffin they had another case of the best clothes, plates and food, on the other side were weapons, if he were a man, and for woman were instruments of their labors. If they were loved so much they were not left alone, the favored slaves were fed and killed to accompany the master.

A little time before the arrival of the Faith in the Islands of Bohol, a group of people called Barangay were killed, food and ammunition were included in the interment. Also included were companions of their exploits. Other burials were done in the fields or under houses where they made fires for several days. They placed watch-towers for they believed that the dead will come back to carry what they left behind.

Lamentation was stopped after the burial and food was served. The drinking and eating continued depending on the status of the dead.

The Spaniards considered the practice of **Pasiam** of the Filipinos curious.

The family of the deceased received donations called ambag to help defray the expense of the burial. This is still practice today. Some were in the form of money, materials, and if the person had none of this, he would give it in the form of service. Far away relatives, friends and neighbors joined them every day and the house was never closed for nine days. They believed that the pain of loss was extreme at night, so they had to distract the pain. These were accompanied with prayers for the reposed soul of the dead. They had to tell stories, legends, and poems to console the spirits.

At midnight events were ended and food was served. The rest had to go home and the relatives of far away places had to stay in the house of the deceased.

The nine days prayers called Pasiam is still a tradition well respected by the Filipino people.

From this point onward it became extremely difficult to fit into a culture of normal category, for their culture was already to a substantial degree. It was unique and unimitable; a uniqueness of many dimensions among which were faith, courtesy, morality, hospitality, etc. a development that amazed the Missionary authors. From the past to the present these are still running like a golden cord.

EPILOGUE

Materially we considered that the early chapters of ancient authors had injured the names of our people especially our ancestors as a result of ignorance and miscomprehension.

These errors might have been copied and transcribed by authors who had not investigated the certainty of what had been written by the preceding authors. The immense work of these authors were considered dogmas by the succeeding authors without taking into account if they were provisional or evidenciary, or if they were not, they omitted to admit some of the narrations of the indigenes.

In every chapter we tried to evade the errors transmitted by putting in its place the narrations of the authors of antiquity like Fathers Chirino, Collin, Morga and others, whose works had little to be impugned.

When these authors implied that the Filipinos were barbaric, uncivilized, ignorant and lazy, they forgot their juridical construction, literature, music, religion, their commerce and industry etc. In these and many works they admitted provoking in them a sensible contradiction in one... of what has been said and on the other another.

Throughout our quest for the pre Spanish civilization, we had the conviction that no one had a right to form opinions that were not based on facts. For these reasons we presented the most profitable fields of observations, citations, narrations and appreciation of merits through accurate analysis. We hope that cynics will have a little self-sacrifice to accept the commendable facts we have presented here, as well as those by both the ancient and modern authors.

Indeed it required a considerable courage and patience for us and the different authors to freely connect facts about our ancient pre-Spanish civilization and to right the wrong that was done to our ancient civilization. With an appreciative understanding will find in our work that a great knowledge of our past had shown the hypothesis of absolute facts.^

News indeed are tiny grains of facts
Separate gossips from facts
They are the blotted archives of the past.
Our growth of grace was high
The blows of fate held us high.
Stand close to truths
There can be no escape from truths
For there's no room for lies
Truths are seen by ears and eyes.

On the other hand many ancient authors were pre-occupied in the exquisite love for truths and debated errors and commented on them, thus facilitating our work.

Finally it is with dignity to account in our favor the ancient civilization of our people, its marvelous and unique culture. It was a proof of its advance progress in the assimilation of the Occidental culture and religion, considered its great attachment to the fondness of their traditions without forgetting the devotion of saintly missionaries in the Christianization of the Philippines and the generosity of Spain.

The outstanding achievements of our forefathers did not receive widespread attention and affection that had characterized it. They were considered mystical stories of ancient authors, written deep into every chapter of their lives. This work substantiated them and unfolded the power behind them.

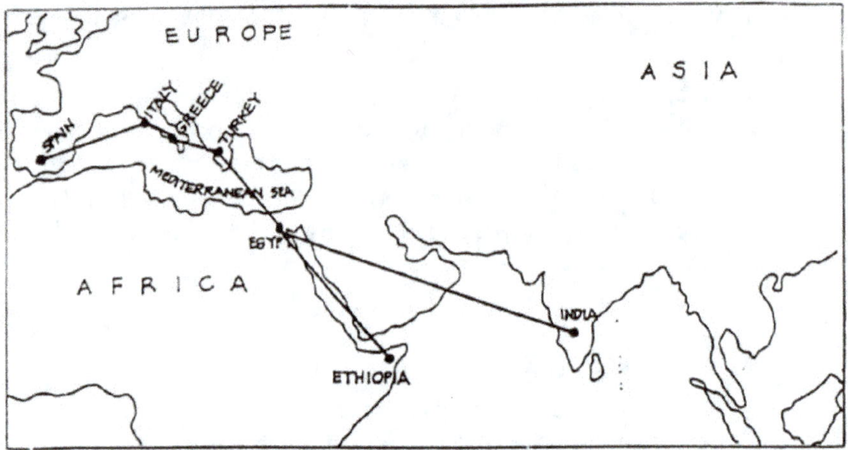

The extent of the Apostle's movement may have covered a vast area extending from Southern Europe in Spain to mainland Asia in India, encompassing the entire civilized regions of the then known world. Thus the claim of the universality of Christianity had a historical basis from the beginning.

AUTHOR'S NOTE

This is a Doctoral Thesis entitled The Pre-Spanish Civilization of the Philippine Archipelago, a pragmatic history in pursuit of truth and the missing historical chronology of our ancient civilization before the arrival of the Spaniards in our lands.

It is a careful analysis of anthologies from annals and chronicles which are primarily important in determining the missing chronology of our ancient civilization. For a history without a chronology is dark and confused; a chronology without a history is dry and insipid."[185]

Although suffering inherent limitation, standing out from the BLUE-PRINTS, are the invaluable historical realities of our sober forefathers in their teeming towns and villages.

But for whom is the work intended? It is for all Filipinos, old and young and those yet to be born, as well as others who, as a consequence of the lack of records had read our history oftentimes misrepresented and therefore had no clear understanding of our ancient past.

In spite of the passage of many centuries the Philippines still hungers for the chronological history of our ancient past, that the anthologist of annals and chronicals had not given birth to it. Nevertheless science had unearth priceless knowledge for the realization of the understanding of our historical hegemony:

(a) The arrival in the Philippines archipelago of Homo Sapiens from the Asian mainland through land bridges during the Pleistocene Era or Ice-age.[186]

(b) The global diaspora of the Hellenistic civilization, where code of morals embodied in the Hellenistic precepts were consciously dispersed.

(c) These historical records proved that inevitably barriers of nations had been broken by human intermediary and these events make these nations allies in the long development of civilization whose center is man's worth.

These historic events were so deep that they were not easily estimated, nevertheless as time prodded on they built their past in the ennobling and uplifting humanity, the sum-total of their achievements from their life's work. These feats were the essential elements and strength were lies the foundation of our civilization,

---

[185] Webster International Dictionary with Reference to Hist. p. 84.
[186] Manila Times 1957

lingering in constancy and continuity and overlooked throughout these past centuries.

The humane culture of our forefathers greatly impressed the first Spanish explorers that they viewed their culture as the background of our civilization. Thus laudable comments were sent to the western world considered as the first news about the existence of our beautiful islands.

It behooves to say that the pioneer days of our forefathers had already passed when the first explorers arrived in the Philippines.

Summarizing them in moral matters we believed that these events were not ordinary happenings or accidents and there were mysteries surrounding this historical phenomenon which differentiated our ancient people from the rest of their peers.

It is perplexing to grasp a view of this legacy of people who were obligated to pursue a special mission, attributes of which gave life its meaning and purpose.

It is difficult to understand our early humane way of life. The explorers said that they saw the insights of Christian living expressed in their actual lives. To have a Christian way of life, it must have the certainty of these facets of God which are love, faith, belief in work, joy, kindness, and peace.

In addition they had concern for others and veered away from self-centeredness. Let us be reminded that there is a nature in man that is vain and selfish. However, our ancient people exhibited fine traits and God-given attributes to the first Spanish explorers who arrived in the Philippines sick and hungry. Our people continue to manifest such traits to this day.

Behind the phenomenon was a Being,
A guide, a companion and a friend.
For a quality of life men has never dreamed.
To make everyone a neighbor and every soul his spiritual kin
That struck much owe and perplexity,
Insights of moral living a filial trusting journey.
Ineridicable points of noble traits,
Blazed with glory and love for others,
A bearing of love in its purest.

"Pre-Spanish Philippines"

WORKS CONSULTED

Fr. Rodrigo de Aganduru – **Historia General de Filipinas.**

Enrique d' Almonte – **Formacion y Evolucion de las Razas Indonesia Malaya.** Madrid, 1917.

Rafael Dias Arenas – **Memorias Historicos y Estadisticos de Filipinas.** Manila, 1850.

Manuel Artigas – **Historia de Filipinas.** Manila, 1916.

David Howard Bain – **Sitting in Darkness (The Americans in the Philippines.**

Fr. Augustine Barreiro – **Estudio Psilogico y Antropologico de la Raza Malayo-Filipina Desde el Dunto de Vieta del Linguaje.** Valladolid, 1910.

Manuel Buceta y Felipe Bravo – **Diccionario Geografico, Estadistico, Historico de las Islas Filipinas.** Madrid, 1851.

Fr. Pedro Chirino – **Relacion de las Islas Filipinas y en lo que Ellas han Trabajado los Padres de la Compania de Jesus.** Roma, 1604. Reimpresa en Manila, 1890.

Domingo Collantes – **Historia de la Provincia de S.S. Rosario,** Manila, 1783.

Fr. Francisco Collin – **Labor Evangelico, Ministerios Apostolicos de los Obreros de Compania de Jesus en Islas Filipinas.** Madrid, 1663.

Francisco Conbes – **Historia de las Islas de Mindanao y Jolo.** Madrid, 1667. Reeditada por Retana en 1897.

Fr. Juan de Concepcion – **Historia General de Filipinas.** Manila y Sampaloc 1788 a 1792.

Balbino Cortes – **Estudio de Archipelago Asiatico** Madrid, 1861.

Felipe Maria de Covamtes – Compendo de la Historia de Filipinas. Manila,1877.

Fr. Juan del Delgado -- **Historia General Sacroprofana, Politica y Natural da las Islas Filipinas.** Manila, 1892.

Enciclopedia Universal Ilustrada – **Espasa Calpe t.23**, Madrid, Bilbao, Barcelona 1924.

Jesus Enciso – **Curso de Historias Comparadas de las Religiones.** Madrid, 1950.

Francisco de Escosura – **Memorias Sobre Filipinas y Jolo.** Madrid 1882.

Juan Fernando y Joaquin Fonseca – **Historias de los P.P. Dominicos en las Islas Filipinas.** Madrid, 1870.

Forman– **The Philippine Islands.** London 1906

Robert B. Fox – **The Tabon Caves-**

Archaeological Explorations and Excavations on Palawan Islands – National Museum. Manila. Official **Journal of the National Geographic Society.** Washington D.C. May, 1988

Msgr. Enrico Galbiate – **History of Salvation in the Old Testament arranged and commented by Msgr. Enrico Galbiate with the help of the Mimep Association.**

Msgr. Enrico Galbiate – **The Early Church in the Acts of the Apostles.**

Msgr. Enrico Galbiate – **The Gospel of Christ – New Edition Text of the Four Gospel arranged into a continuous narrative prepared by the Members of the Mimep.**

Reymondo G. Getll – **Historias de las Ideas Politicas** (Tradiccion de Teodoro Gonzales Garcia). Barcelona, 1950.

Juan de Grijava – **Cronica de la Orden de San Agustin.** Mejico, 1634.

Michael Habarlandt – **Etnografia** (tradiccion de T. Aranzadi)

Herman Hagedorn – Edited – **The Free Citizen** By Pres. Roosevelt.

Napoleon Hill – **The Law of Success.**

Felix Huertas – **Estado Geografico, Topografico, Estadistico,**

Religioso de la Provincia de Religiosos de San Francisco. Manila, 1855. Binondo, 1865.

E.Jacquet – **Consideration sur les Alphabets de Philippines.** Paris, 1831. **Les Philippines:**

Histoire Geographie, Moeurs Agriculture, Industrie. Paris, 1846.

Ramon Jordana y Morera-Bosquejo – **Geografico y Historico del Archipelago Filipino.** Madrid, 1885.

Stanley Kaenov – **Catholic Magazine** based reporter.

Sotero Laurel – **Manila Times.**

Ventura Fernandes Lopez – **La Religion de los Antiguos Indios Tagalogs.** Madrid, 1894.

Fr. Cipriano Marcilla – **Estudios de los Antiguos Alfabetos de Filipinas.** Malabon, 1895

Fr. Domingo Martines-**Compendo Apostolico Provincia ce de Filipinas.** 1756.

Sinibaldo Mas – **Informe de las Islas Filipinas.** 1842

Toribio Miguel – **Unidad de la Especie Humana Probada por la Filologia.** Madrid, 1889.

Claudio Montero – **Boletin de la Sociedad Geografica.** Madrid 1876.

Morga - **Susesos en las Islas Filipinas.**

Fernandez de Navarrete- **Tratado s Historicos.**

Pedro M. Paterno - **La Antigua Civilization Tagala.** Madrid 1887.

Antonio Pigafetta - **Primo Viaje en Torno al Globo Terraqueo,** Corredato di Notte de Carlo Amoteti. Milano, 1800. Hemos utizado la edicion espanola de E. Calpe. Madrid, 1922.

W.E. Retena – **Los Antiguos Alfabetos de Filipinas.** 1875

W.E. Retana – **Supersticiones de los Indios Filipinos.**

Isabelo de los Reyes – **Las Visayas en la Epoca de la Conquista**

Iloilo, 1877.

Roberson – **Bibliography of the Philippines.** Cleveland, 1908.

Vicente de Salazar – **Historia de la Proviciana de Santisimo Rosario de Filipinas.** Manila, 1749.

W.E. Retana – **Bibliografico de la Historica General de Filipinas**

Fr. Juan Francisco de San Antonio – **Cronicas de la Apostolica Provincia de San Gregorio Magno de los Religiosos Descalzos de San Francisco en las Islas Filipinas.** Sampaloc 1748-1744.

W.E. Sangester – **The Secret of Radiant Life**

Fr. Andres de San Nicolas – **Historia General de las Islas Filipinas de los Descalzos de la Orden de San Agustin.** Madrid, 1644.

Agustin Santayana – **La Isla de Midanao, Su Historia,** Madrid 1863.

Fr. Francisco de Santa Ines – **Cronica de San Gregorio Magno de los Religiosos Descalzos de San Francisco en las Filipinas.** Manila, 1892.

Manuel Scheidnagel – **El Archipelago de Legaspi.** Manila 1890.

Manuel Scheidnagel – **Las Colonias Espaniolas en Asia. Madrid,** 1870.

T.H. Pardo de Tavera – **El Sanscrito en la Lengua Tagalog.** Paris 1887

Fr. Pedro Murillo Velarde – **Carta Geografica de las Islas Filipinas.** Manila, 1735.

Jose Monter Vidal – **El Archipelago Filipino.** Madrid, 1886.

F. Ramon Martinez Vigil – **La Escritura Propia de los Tagalogs.** Revista de Filipinas. Manila 1876

Gregorio F. Zaide – **The Philippines Since Pre-Spanish Times.** Manila.

Fr. Joaquin Martines de Zuniga – **Historias de las Islas Filipinas. Sampaloc,** 1903

Index

The fascinating Malicong rice terraces
before the planting season. Mt. Province

ABOUT THE AUTHOR

Juana Jimenez Pelmoka was born in Penaranda, Nueva Ecija. As a young child of a widowed mother, they immigrated to Muñoz, Nueva Ecija where she grew up and eventually married the first lawyer of the town.

In her early years as a public school teacher, she dreamt of rendering a better service to her country. A graduate of the Institute of Spanish of Letran College, she received her doctorate in Roman Philology from the Central Universidad de Madrid in Spain.

At the National Library of Madrid Spain she pored over priceless secrets and startling truths about the ancient histories of the world and gathered epochal materials for the enlightening chronology of the evolution of Philippine civilization. She wrote this book to render a better service to her country.

College of San Juan de Letran

Un Honor Para El
Instituto de Español

Dra. Juana J. de Pelmoka

La Dra. Juana Jiménez de Pelmoka, una de los productos de nuestro Instituto de Español, llegó recientemente de España. La doctora es la estudiante del Instituto que, poco después de obtener su título de A.B. en marzo de 1955, se marchó a Madrid para cursar estudios superiores en la Universidad Central de Madrid, Facultad de Filosofía y Letras (sección de Lenguas). Terminó el curso de doctor en un año. El título de su tesis es: LA CIVILIZACION DE FILIPINAS PRE-HISPANICA.

La Dra. de Pelmoka es la primera alumna del Instituto que ha obtenido el título de doctor, y nada menos que en España. Su logro es un alto honor tanto para el Instituto como para el Colegio.

Como señal de su profundo cariño, regaló al Instituto una copia de su tesis doctoral.

River and the Mayon Volcano
Philippines

Philippine fruits

Philippine Parrots